Tony Hawk – Footplant, 1982.
Photo © J. Grant Brittain

Sylvie Barco
Philippe Danjean
Stéphane Madoeuf

Skateboarding's urban heritage

THE ART OF SKATEBOARDING

CASSELL

The equipment required may be simple, but skateboarding is about far more than just a board and four wheels, the proof being the passion and creativity it continues to arouse among its followers today. Skateboarding is a culture in its own right, with its high points, its heroes and technical prowess demonstrated in the street and dedicated skating spaces, but it also exists through its own unique artistic expression. We'll explore its rich history, revealing its modest origins, its evolution and its close connection with the worlds of fashion and design.

This is a journey full of adventure, across decades of evolution and change, from the first rudimentary boards to the emergence of a thriving industry boasting iconic brands and distinctive styles, with forays into the world of video games and increasingly frequent crossovers with music, cinema and photography. We examine how skateboarding has captured the heart of society and established itself as a cultural force in its own right, with dedicated showcase events, exhibitions and festivals, even attaining the status of an Olympic sport in the process!

This is confirmation for a discipline that grew up on the streets and, despite the creation of skateparks more or less everywhere in the world, continues to evolve in improvised spaces.

Finally, Sylvie Barco's photographic series entitled *Gang of Skate* and its accompanying text capture as closely as possible the fleeting moments that define this playful but athletic discipline in which ideas of cultural transmission and a sense of belonging to a community play a crucial role.

Our hope in publishing this book is to capture the essence of skateboarding as a living, breathing cultural movement in which art, freedom and a powerful sense of community converge to create a unique human experience.

INTRODUCTION

H&W LANDSCAPE SERVICES

CONTENTS

< Steve Steadham and Mike McGill, 1965.
Photo © J. Grant Brittain

A BRIEF HISTORY OF SKATEBOARDING

The Geneva Skateboard Museum.
Photo © Nicolas Barthélémy

FROM THE ROOTS OF SKATEBOARDING TO THE EMERGENCE OF A NEW WAVE

It is impossible to attribute the birth of skateboarding to anyone in particular. The story goes that it first appeared in the surfing hotspots of California and Hawaii during the 1950s, when a summer without wind and waves drove surfers to fix wheels to the bottom of their boards to reduce the friction of 'sidewalk surfing'.

The cover of *Surfing* magazine, December 1969.

Still taken from Bruce Brown's film *Barefoot Adventure*, 1960.

> 'WE WERE SKATING ON CONCRETE WAVES'
>
> **Tony Alva**

IN THE (VERY) BEGINNING

The origins of skateboarding in fact go right back to roller-skating, which had been relatively widespread in the United States from the 19th century until the advent of the kick scooter in the 1930s. This is not the whole story, however. Intimately linked with the sensation of gliding, skateboarding definitely owes something to other sports, particularly water-skiing and downhill skiing, which had caught the public imagination and had seen numbers of enthusiasts skyrocket in the 1960s and 1970s. During this period, skateboarding relied on equipment (now known as 'surf skates') that was entirely earthbound. It had yet to take to the skies.

A hybrid scooter/skateboard, undated.
© Mucem

A prototype 'snow skateboard', 1975.
Photo © Leyla Madoeuf

Techni-ski skateboard, 1972, The Geneva Skateboard Museum.
Photo © Leyla Madoeuf

Roller Derby became the first commercial skateboard manufacturers in 1959.
© Mucem

Techni-ski advertisement, 1972, The Geneva Skateboard Museum.
Photo © Nicolas Barthélémy

Images taken from Claude Jutra's film *The Devil's Toy*, 1966.

The 1966 Canadian documentary *The Devil's Toy* by the director Claude Jutra featured one of the first attempts to describe this new craze and is revealing in more ways than one. It not only shows young people racing down the streets of Montreal on the first skateboards (pulling off moves that have more to do with skiing than surfing) but also captures the boundless energy of these young skating devotees who were attracting increasing hostility from the municipal authorities. The film opens with a dedication to 'all victims of intolerance', illustrating the director's opposition to a self-righteous society unable to tolerate the freedom that these young people were enjoying.

'Two hundred years of American technology has unwittingly created a massive cement playground of unlimited potential. But it was the minds of 11-year-olds that could see that potential.'[1]

In terms of equipment, while the dawn of skateboarding saw handmade boards with no branding, logos or designs, and each skater customizing the board as they saw fit, significant improvements were inevitable as the sport evolved. DIY gradually developed into a cottage industry and was then replaced by the beginnings of commercialization.

The advent of standardization was closely followed by the first sporting events, and the first competition, held in Hermosa Beach (a suburb city of Los Angeles, California) in 1963, saw competitors face off in various ground-based events such as slalom and freestyle. The quality of a trick was judged on its difficulty and novelty, but most importantly on its artistic appeal. The first French competition took place in 1965 and Arnaud de Rosnay, a photographer, surfer and adventurer who went missing in 1984, was victorious for the first three years running.

Drawing on a still modestly sized base of enthusiasts, skateboarding was able to take its first baby steps and see a whole ecosystem develop to encourage its evolution.

1 C.R. Stecyk, 'Aspects of the Downhill Slide', *Skateboarder Magazine*, vol. 2, no. 2, 1975.

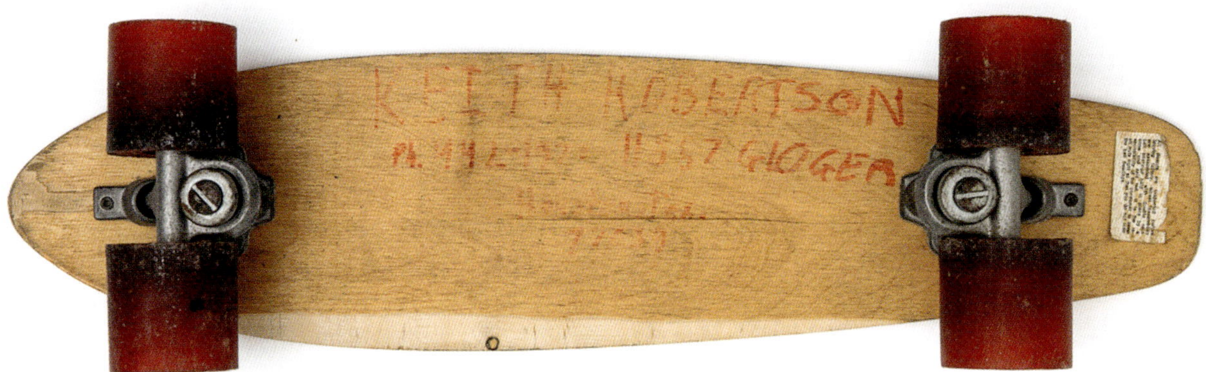

Roller Derby no. 20 de luxe, late 1960s.
Photo © Nicolas Scordia

A room in The Geneva Skateboard Museum.
Photo © Nicolas Barthélémy

February 1978. Vol. 2. No. 10

National Skateboard

REVIEW

HOBIE SKATEBOARDS

BOB SKILDBERG, Hobie team Professional, setting up early through the critical offset section in the Giant Slalom. Skolbie held the best speed line through this section earning him 1st Place in the Hester 500 Challenge. Excellant day for the L.C.B. Pro!

National Skateboard Review, 1978.

INDUSTRIALIZATION

Respect to those early pioneers. This is where it all began and where it all took off. The first skate shop opened its doors in Hollywood in 1962, selling homemade skateboards, and this first tentative step towards commercial manufacturing opened the door for a whole new generation of skaters to try their hand at the sport.

The very first advertisement appeared a year later in *Surf Guide Magazine* (which was dedicated to surfing), while *The Quarterly Skateboarder*, the first specialist magazine, was launched in 1964.

Equipment was constantly evolving during this period as it adapted to the changing needs of riders. Wheels, originally made of metal, were now being produced in clay, which certainly made for a more comfortable ride. Production soared, with more than 50 million boards sold in the United States in three years, directly resulting in an oversupply of poor-quality decks, while the number of bans on skateboarding in cities and towns kept pace with this. It goes some way towards explaining the relative decline of the sport in 1965, although it was to experience a real renaissance at the end of this period thanks to several key developments. It is telling that the first brand of shoes created by a skater for skaters was to come from the factories of the Vans company as the firm jumped on the emerging bandwagon in 1966.

'Let's challenge' surfskate.
Photo © Nicolas Scordia

Making urethane wheels.
© Division of Culture and the Arts, National Museum of American History, Smithsonian Institution

A typical plastic board from the 1970s.
Photo © Nicolas Scordia

The first innovation came at the turn of the 1970s with the introduction of urethane wheels, which were more comfortable for skating and versatile. Skateboarding was also greatly influenced by the evolution in technology during the famous 'age of plastic'. This new material was to help reduce manufacturing costs and so facilitate exports, with the first American boards crossing the Atlantic in 1976.

The creation of new types of boards also played a key role in the resurgence of skateboarding, with a growth in popularity of shorter boards that are easier to handle and flip (now often referred to as 'old school boards'). This made them more suited to stunts and tricks than the longer, stiffer boards of previous years.

Curt Kimbel in La Costa, 1977.
Photo © Jim Goodrich

Jay Adams in the mid-1970s. >
© D.R.

TURN
ONLY

Tony Alva, Malibu, 1979.
Photo © Jim Goodrich

TAKING FLIGHT

Regardless of the type of board, by 1969 skaters had begun to colonize the playgrounds of the schools built along the hillsides surrounding Santa Monica, where the sloping terrain provided an alternative to the waves and rollers of the ocean. As mentioned, surf culture had played a defining role in the popularization of this new activity. Many skaters of the time were also surfers who brought their characteristic style and moves to skateboarding. So what prompted this transition from ocean to asphalt? Once again, this was weather related.

A great drought hit the West Coast of the United States at the turn of the 1970s; the concrete channel of the Los Angeles River dried out beneath the city's bridges and residents were forced to drain their swimming pools. Skaters took over these new and unexpected spaces, sometimes illegally venturing into certain residential areas where particularly beautiful swimming pools were located. This marked the beginning of the 'vert' (vertical) skating that is now echoed in the ramps seen in skateparks, in what ultimately is an attempt to imitate the curves of the pools that were strongly reminiscent of waves. 'Carving', a technique of skating in fluid arcs that imitated the movements of a wave, soon became cool.

A few brand logos featured on boards during this decade, but very few were decorated with graphics. The top of the board was now covered with 'grip', a rough surface that gave better traction. As far as graphics were concerned, brand images were being developed, but appearing primarily on clothing and in advertising.

Competitions eventually began to emerge, giving skaters a chance to test themselves against one another and showcase their talents. Events such as the Del Mar Nationals in California and the Super Bowl Skateboarding Contest in Florida in 1975 helped to promote skateboarding and drum up media attention. At the same time, professionalism in the sport was on the rise and a recognized scene began to emerge, with names such as Tony Alva, Stacy Peralta and Jay Adams (known as the 'Z-Boys') pulling off previously unimaginable tricks before the appearance of Tony Hawk, a future skating legend, in the late 1970s.

Stacy Peralta, Upland, 1978.
Photo © Jim Goodrich

Steve Caballero, 1985.
Photo © Jim Goodrich

Skateboarding was no longer simply a matter of appropriating existing spaces. Looking to 'catch waves' in concrete by quite literally reproducing surfing moves meant adapting the skater's motion to the curves of a hard surface in the hope of finding a little of the freedom and power provided by watersports. Skateboarding originated in appropriation – borrowing both equipment and urban space to create a unique and innovative sporting discipline that was transcending the bounds of the specific circumstances in which it had evolved.

There are so many reasons why this period between 1976 and 1980 is often considered one of the most important eras in the history of skateboarding.

Press photo of a young New Yorker in the mid-1980s.
D.R.

G&S team in a flower bowl, 1977. >
Photo © Jim Goodrich

Hobie

Central Park, New York, 1979.

THE 80S
BOARDS COME OUT OF THE SHADOWS

This was the decade when skateboarding was at the height of its popularity, especially among young people, when its entire universe underwent transformation and development in terms of brands, styles and competitions – nothing escaped the winds of change!

NEW TRICKS, NEW IMAGE

Skaters started to experiment with new tricks and ever more daring moves such as the 'ollie', which propels the board into the air with a stomp, or the 'kickflip', which spins the board beneath the feet. The ollie, invented by Rodney 'Ollie' Mullen, represented a real departure from previous techniques. Riding on ramps was no longer the only way to take off and the street suddenly became a new playground. It marked a real paradigm shift in riders' perception of their environment: a sidewalk, a step or a bench had suddenly become a new way to find self-expression.

The nuisance in terms of noise and damage to street furniture led to a public outcry. More and more cities introduced skating bans, and riders began to ignore them just as quickly. Brands moved fast to exploit this state of affairs and reach an adolescent audience attracted to a hobby that suddenly seemed subversive. In the mid-1980s, the Powell Peralta brand published an advertisment with the tagline 'skateboarding is not a crime'. The slogan was picked up everywhere, despite the minor detail that skateboarding had never actually been criminally penalized.

• A 'Pulp68' branded patch.
© The Geneva Skateboard Museum

• Felix Jonsson jumping over a prohibition sign.
Photo © Jim Goodrich

• A typical 'No Skating' sign.
© Division of Culture and the Arts, National Museum of American History, Smithsonian Institution

The artistic direction taken in these years by the skateboarding industry would lead to an inadvertent alignment with the worlds of punk, hard rock and graffiti. The monthly magazine *Thrasher* hit American newsstands in 1981 and in editorial terms was also very rock-oriented. Skating articles and photos, along with interviews and information about skateparks and music, are its stock in trade. The introduction of a range of streetwear featuring its famous flame logo only served to increase the magazine's popularity. This was followed two years later by the launch of *Trans-world*, an equally influential magazine.

This shift towards a more rebellious and aggressive (not to mention highly gendered) image would also result in an under-representation of female skating in the media. This was all too typical for the time, and the upshot was a significant slowdown in the number of women getting involved in the sport.

Cover of *Trans-world Skateboarding* magazine, 1983.

The classic 'Slasher' character (1987) and a clone with the face of Bart Simpson to mark the 500th episode (2012); boards designed by Jim Phillips for the Santa Cruz brand.

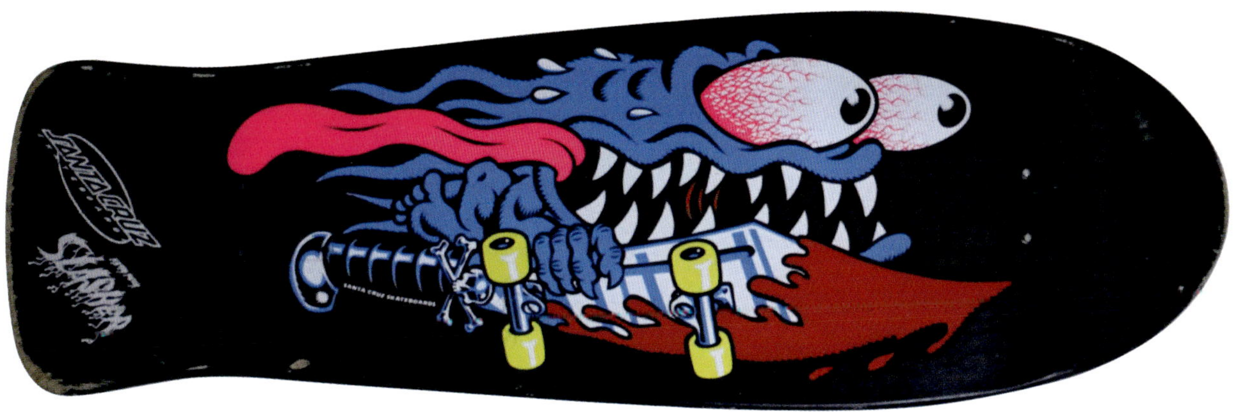

A NEW GENERATION OF BOARDS

Taking to the air with vert skating in the empty swimming pools of the 1970s allowed riders to spread their wings, but the photos of the time were also to reveal something new: the underside of the board. Brands were quick to realize the enormous communications potential of this and began to produce designs and series after series of printed images. These graphics soon became hugely important, with a strong preference for 'dragon' and 'skull' motifs, symbols that also resonated with the 'punk' reputation the scene had recently acquired.

Some artists began to make a real name for themselves, however, including Jim Phillips and Wes Humpston, whose Dogtown boards were hand-painted for the Z-Boys crew.

A poster collage of Jim Phillips's graphical creations for the skateboarding industry. >

JEFF
KENDALL
INDEPEND
SLIME
BALLS
OLLIE ON A DIME! · OJ II ELITES ·
Elites
METHOD AIR ON A DARE · OJ II ·
OJ II ELITE
SANTA CR

CRUZ
SKATEBOARDS
SPEED WHEELS
NATAS
SANTA MONICA
AIRLINES
SANTA CRUZ

Jim Phillips famously created the logo for the Independent Truck Company brand, which, by 1978, was manufacturing nearly 50 per cent of all the trucks – the axle assemblies fitted to the base of the board – in the country and supplying the finest skaters of the era, along with a multitude of designs for the Santa Cruz brand. These included the Rob Roskopp series and the iconic severed blue hand with its screaming mouth. In 1987, he unveiled 'Slasher', a blue creature with eyes out on stalks, armed with a large bloodied knife, who became one of the Santa Cruz brand's symbolic figures, and designed what was known as a 'pro model' for the skater Natas. There are several critical points in the life of a skater, but turning professional is invariably marked by the production of a branded board (with the new professional's name and image on it) that fans can buy for themselves.

In the wake of all this upheaval came the establishment of major sporting competitions such as the Skateboard World Championships and the X Games, get-togethers and rallies that have become unmissable for certain professional skaters and are still being held across the continents to this day.

Boards featuring Jim Phillips's design for the skater Natas, The Geneva Skateboard Museum.
Photo © Nicolas Barthélémy

Portrait of Natas with his pro board at Sanoland.
Photo © J. Grant Brittain

A Powell Peralta-branded pro skateboard signed by the skater Tony Hawk.
© Mucem

Tony Hawk. >
Photo © J. Grant Brittain

10 FOOT BONE LESS
CARLSBAD PIPELINES

THE

WHEN DESIGN TOOK OVER SKATING

The 1990s were a pivotal period for skateboarding culture. This was a decade in which riders continued to push the envelope of creativity, in particular by inventing new tricks and techniques that would inspire generations to come.

Chet Thomas, San Diego. >
Photo © J. Grant Brittain

SKATING
CYCLING
T FOR
ATIONAL USE

Portrait photo of Tony Hawk.
Division of Culture and the Arts, National Museum of American History, Smithsonian Institution/ Photo © Rick Chapman

HIGHER AND HIGHER

The decks from this decade were smaller and lighter than those of previous years, making them easier to handle and attempt all kinds of daring tricks. Street skateboarding was skyrocketing in popularity and this new style soon allied itself to the emergent hip-hop scene, which had its roots in the same environment. Vert skateboarding became super popular, which showcased aerial tricks and technical skills on a U-shaped ramp with walls about 15ft (4.5m) high.

The creation of major events was an opportunity for riders to compete against one another, show off their skills and make a name for themselves. America's Tony Hawk, now considered a skateboarding legend, transformed the 'vert' style with an iconic trick known as the '900', which he unveiled for the first time at the X Games in 1999. It consisted of a 2½ aerial revolution (one rotation with an angle of 360° + 360° + 180°). This achievement earned him legions of fans and he was to star in a PlayStation video game the same year. He went on to establish the Tony Hawk Foundation several years later, opening some 500 skateparks in deprived areas.

The 1990s also witnessed significant progress in developing spaces specifically designed for skateboarding, with elements often mimicking urban street architecture and playing with curved lines and ramps. These custom-made structures helped to free up the sidewalks from skaters who were becoming increasingly daring and provided them with a slightly more supervised playground.

Tony Hawk, aged 16, in 1984.
Photo © Jim Goodrich

A MOVEMENT IN SEARCH OF AN IDENTITY

Despite all this progress, however, it should be remembered that the general public remained if not hostile, then at least highly critical. The sport was still a fringe pursuit and turning professional remained an impossible dream for a great many skaters. During these years in particular, skateboarding was an activity in search of an identity. Social media did not yet exist, and the big brands and large-scale kit retailers (such as Adidas and Nike) were still not interested in the market. It was during this very specific period that a raw, authentic culture emerged, untouched by outside influences, creating a unique era that some regard as the golden age of the movement.

With their striking designs and bright graphics, the boards of the 1990s represented a turning point in the look of skateboards as the sport broke away from the punk and hard rock designs of the 1980s. The exhibition *Art of Skate* (Paris, Fluctuart 2022) featured a trio of boards signed by America's Marc McKee, one of the greatest board designers of the 1990s, whom Jim Zbinden, founder of The Geneva Skateboard Museum, considers to be the most influential graphic artist of this new wave.

One board entitled *Accidental gun* has become truly emblematic for its graphic, violent imagery satirizing the right to bear arms and its consequences in the United States. These radical images tended strongly towards the polemical, and their message might seem highly disturbing. 'Marc McKee's art was so controversial,' recalls Rodney Mullen, another legendary skater of the era, 'that they had an entire wall of Cease and Desist orders for his graphics at World Industries.[2]'

Just as the technical prowess of the pioneers of the 1990s was to have lasting effects on the skaters who were to follow, the unique designs and vivid graphics of the skateboards of the time remained an essential reference point for modern riders and many contemporary artists.

2 World Industries was founded by Steve Rocco and Rodney Mullen in 1987 as one of the first skateboarding companies to be both owned and operated by professional skaters.

Boards designed by Marc McKee, The Geneva Skateboard Museum.
Photo © Leyla Madoeuf

'MARC MCKEE'S ART WAS SO CONTROVERSIAL THAT THEY HAD AN ENTIRE WALL OF CEASE AND DESIST ORDERS'

Rodney Mullen

THE BIRTH OF AN INDUSTRY

BRANDS, LOOKS AND VIDEO GAMES

Skateboarding continued to evolve throughout the 2000s as brands proliferated, each one bringing its own unique look and identity.

THE BOOM

Skateboarding was becoming popular on a global scale and the number of skaters skyrocketed. The internet spread vast quantities of images and videos, hugely accelerating this unprecedented expansion. The sport also began to feature regularly in video games as new options were released, including three supplementary packs for the *Tony Hawk Pro Skater* game on PlayStation.

Big brands and equipment suppliers finally took notice of the opportunities offered by this booming market and began to take a closer look. Nike launched its skateboarding range in 2002, followed by Adidas in 2006. The skateboarding industry was spreading its wings.

This expansion naturally came with new influences, and clothing styles evolved accordingly. Although the fashion references of the 1990s (baggy pants and T-shirts) remained relevant, this pivotal era was to shape the unique identity of skateboarding. Borrowing from urban culture and hip-hop, the brand's loose jeans and outsize T-shirts started to attract the attention of the uninitiated.

The PlayStation 1 console was launched in the mid-1990s with the games *Thrasher: Skate & Destroy* and *Tony Hawk's Skateboarding.*
Photo © Nicolas Scordia

CREATIVITY FIRING ON FOUR CYLINDERS

Board design has been considered a true skateboarding art ever since the early 2000s. The graphics themselves were affected by this new wave of creativity, unleashing total freedom of expression. New printing technology made it possible to design boards and bring new models onto the market on a regular basis, and manufacturers competed in inventiveness in order to stand out from the crowd. There was no longer any one style or particularly recurring motifs, although the pro model system remained relevant and resonated with a wider public as the 'star system' encouraged partnerships with professional riders and boosted their incomes.

The Japanese artist Haroshi was pushing the envelope of artistic expression as early as 2005, not only reinterpreting skateboards as used by subcultures but also recycling old boards, which he styled to follow contemporary branding.

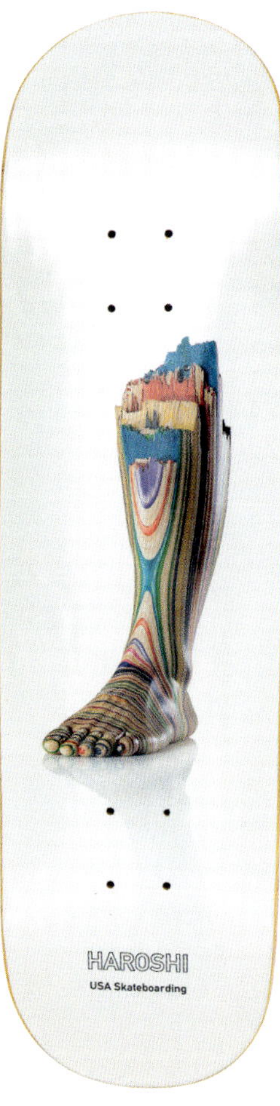

From left to right: Yoshito Nara for MoMa New York; the photographer Larry Clark on the occasion of one of his exhibitions with the United Arrows brand; James Joyce reinterprets the smiley for Colette; Haroshi marks the inclusion of skateboarding at the 2020 Olympic Games.
Photo © Nicolas Scordia

The American photographer Martha Cooper, who has achieved global renown for her work with graffiti, chose this image entitled *Leap of Faith* from her 1978 album *On the Street* to be reworked by the American street artist Shepard Fairey as a stencil for screen printing. The image first featured on a skateboard in a run from 2009.
© Martha Cooper/© Shepard Fairey/Photo © Nicolas Scordia

Hip-hop celebrated its tenth birthday in 1983 and Charlie Ahearn's film *Wild Style* documented the history of B-boys and the birth of graffiti in New York. This historic photo of Lil Crazy Legs, taken by Martha Cooper on the film set, also appears on the cover of her book *Hip Hop Files*.
© Martha Cooper/Photo © Nicolas Scordia

DIFFERENT DISCIPLINES

There are a host of different approaches to skateboarding nowadays, and the evolution of the sport from the 1960s to the present day reflects the apparently limitless possibilities.

From the moment a would-be skater first picks up a board, there are no rules, no instructions and no order in which to learn the tricks, giving a sense of complete freedom that not only makes every skater unique but also promotes the exchange of ideas between the different disciplines. Some moves have come to dominate, however, uniting both 'street' and 'bowl' skaters, although 'vert' should also not be forgotten.

These terms describe both the different approaches to skating and the places where they are practiced, once again highlighting the importance of the rider's immediate surroundings.

< Jeroen Bruggeman, 2022.
Photo © Gabriel Renault

STREET

This is the most widespread style and with good reason – it is what truly popularized skateboarding. Real 'street' riding is carried out on the streets – the skater has to pick their spot and then work with the urban architecture they find there, or go to a skatepark that reproduces the urban environment with various features such as rails, jumps, slopes...

Juan Renoux pulling off a crooked grind during the Erotic Hill Bomb in Paris, 2023. Taking place on streets with slopes perfect for downhill skateboarding, the event, orchestrated by Crew Erotic, celebrated skateboarding, art and culture, while pushing the boundaries of personal expression in an urban environment.
Photo © Jeff 'Suds' Sudmeier

< James Woodley doing a 360 flip.
Photo © Jeff 'Suds' Sudmeier

BOWL OR 'POOL'

Named after the hollowed-out, enclosed space used for skateboarding, the bowl is a direct descendant of early skating in the empty swimming pools of LA in the 1970s. It is now an Olympic discipline (incorrectly known as 'park' – a skatepark being, by definition, a place specifically dedicated to skateboarding, with the moves possible depending directly on its architecture). A bowl is a skatepark by nature, but the term is also used for what could be termed a street-style space, which is an area where items of street furniture (steps, rails, benches, etc.) have been reproduced for skaters to perform series of tricks (this is also an Olympic discipline, improperly named 'street').

Martin Leclair at Venice Beach, California.
Photo © Jeff 'Suds' Sudmeier

Martin Leclair at Venice Beach, California. >
Photo © Nicolas Jacquemin

VERT

Vert or vertical skateboarding describes a method of skating that makes use of a large, U-shaped ramp with vertical walls, 15ft (4.5m) (or more) high. It was this discipline that famously made Tony Hawk's name as an iconic sports and video games legend. There was perhaps limited enthusiasm for the sport in France due to a lack of suitable infrastructure, but this did not stop Frenchman Édouard Damestoy from winning the X Games in 2023.

Vert skating at Barneville's Gliss Festival, Normandy, France, 2022.
Courtesy of Mauna Kea Organisation

Shani Bru in the vert competition, Hangar Darwin skatepark, Bordeaux. >
Photo © Fred Ferrand

TO BE OR NOT TO BE
IN THE OLYMPIC SYSTEM

Having been included in the 2014 Youth Olympic Games, skateboarding made its debut in the traditional form of the Olympics in Tokyo in 2021 (officially the 2020 Olympics) with a male and female event in each discipline. Performances were judged according to technical criteria rating creativity, difficulty and fluidity.

The advent of skateboarding as an Olympic discipline was born from the organizers' wish to attract a younger audience to the Games, by showcasing urban styles and habits.

Board signed by the American team for the debut of skateboarding at the 2020 Olympic Games in Tokyo.

The recent adoption of skateboarding by the Olympics has caused much debate among skaters. For some it is first and foremost a fun activity, a whole culture, a means of expression and freedom, which the institutionalization represented by inclusion in the Games can only threaten and derail.

There are already a number of well-publicized competitions but there are not really any titles at stake (in fact, few skaters would be able to name the world champion). Before the Olympics, there had never been a competition in skateboarding in which countries directly competed with one another.

A large number of professional skaters (particularly street skaters) decline to take part in competitions and are more interested in making videos or shooting photos than competing in championships or similarly competitive events. Since its very beginnings, there has been a high level of photographic documentation, and a substantial stock of iconic images is available.

So it might seem perplexing when events are not filmed by the skaters who actually feature in the images, and this was one of the recurring criticisms of these first Games in 2021, where many of the image-framing choices could be seen as questionable.

Another frequently asked question related to the choice of a temporary skatepark on the Place de la Concorde in Paris for the 2024 Olympic Games. Aside from the environmental considerations, there is currently no permanent infrastructure of this kind in Paris and the Olympiad could have been an opportunity to construct such a facility in the city or its suburbs.

Lastly, there has been much debate about the high price of tickets and the exclusive advertising provided for the benefit of the big brands, two major aspects that are not part of skateboarding culture.

Despite these limitations, the institutionalization of skateboarding has made it more acceptable to many cities, and bans and anti-skating measures are becoming increasingly rare. A new attitude is becoming apparent in the construction of skateparks, the organization of events and help in setting up dedicated schools for the discipline. Similarly, recognition of skaters as top-level athletes and as members of their national teams is revolutionary and clear proof of profound change. The Olympics may also be a way of increasing the number of women and girls involved in the sport, as women's skateboarding remains all too frequently underpublicized.

While the Olympic Games might not be an entirely faithful reflection of the true essence of skating, skaters have no doubt that the intrinsic authenticity of their beloved sport is too powerful and too firmly rooted in their minds to be endangered by this recent formalization.

Double-page spread from a Japanese magazine documenting the victory of two young Japanese hopefuls in the Women's Park event at the 2020 Olympic Games; the average age on the medal podium was 15. >

Photo © Nicolas Scordia

スポニチ

東京五輪 第13日 4日

スケートボード 女子パーク 有明アーバンスポーツパーク

スケボーニッポン 五輪で女子初の表彰台ワンツー

19歳 四十住（よそずみ）金

季節外れでも鮮やかに“さくら”咲き誇りました

スポーツニッポン

2021年8月5日【木】 11版A

いま、その輝きに、乾杯！

五輪特集 完全ガイド 記録集 写真集 抜き取り4ページ

週末は往復5時間 学校終わりに往復3時間 母の運転で技を磨いて

女子パークは四十住（よそずみ）さくら（19＝ベンヌ）が60・09点で初代女王に輝いた。12歳の開心那（ひらき・ここな、WHYDAH GROUP）は銀メダルを獲得し、大会4日目に女子ストリートを13歳で制した西矢椛（もみじ、ムラサキスポーツ）を超えて日本史上最年少メダリストとなった。日本女子の五輪ワンツーは初。世界ランキング1位の岡本碧優（みすぐ、15＝MKグループ）は4位だった。新競技のスケートボードは男女ストリートと合わせて3種目を日本勢が制し、新たなお家芸の地位を確立した。【関係記事5・共競面】

大勝負「540」×2

親の願いと娘の情熱

重さを胸に3年後へ

◇女子パーク決勝成績◇

堀米＆西矢W頂点の「ストリート」に続いて日の丸躍動

よそずみ 四十住さくら ハイチュウ大好き 激レア全国に180人

ひらき ここな 開心那 南国好きの母が命名「ココナツ」

今日は何の日？（8月5日）

Sponichi TOKYO 2020

12歳最年少 開心那（ひらき・ここな） 銀

10代少女が

メダルとか 年齢とか 3年後とか そんなことより「格好いいかどうか」

スケートボード女子パークで銀メダルを獲得した開（撮影・小海途 良幹） ①②笑顔で日の丸を掲げる金メダルの四十住（右）と銀メダルの開

岩崎恭子超えた西矢椛を超えた 世界歴代年少7位12歳343日

スケートボード女子パークで12歳343日の開心那が銀メダルを獲得した。メダリストとしては今大会競技女子ストリート金の西矢椛が記録した13歳330日を更新し、日本歴代最年少となった。

スケボーに熱中しすぎて…「自転車に乗れない」

札幌の練習場・高木店長が語る開

開の地元・北海道にある札幌市の練習施設「HOT BOWL skate park」の関係者約70人が市内体育館での応援会で声援を送った。銀メダル獲得が決まると「心那、よく頑張った」と歓喜に包まれた。

同施設で店長を務める高木秀昭さんは、小1から同施設に週3、4回通っている開について「最初はみんながいる中の一人、という感じ」と印象を語る。飛び抜けた才能があったわけではないが、母や祖母のお手製弁当を持参し休むことも忘れて5、6時間は練習に没頭。「練習量が物おじしないことにつながる。真面目。本当に凄いと思う」と舌を巻く。

……ついて「（スケボーに没頭するあまりに）自転車にも乗れない。ここで練習していますよ」とこっそり明かした。

3位ブラウンは日本生まれ　4位は岡本　新競技だけど　すっかりお家芸

WHEN THE UNDERGROUND BECOMES MAINSTREAM CULTURE

Erotic Hill Bomb, 2023.
Photo © Jeff 'Suds' Sudmeier

THE SKATEBOARDING SHOE INDUSTRY

The first archive photos of skateboarding show many skaters riding barefoot, such as in images captured by Hugh Holland in 1970. This originated in the Californian scene and was rooted in the era's surfing and beach life – even hippy – mindset of the time. It featured on the famous cover of *LIFE* magazine from 1965, with the iconic photo of Patti McGee.

For reasons of both practicality and comfort, however, skateboarders had to adopt footwear that would suit their new passion. In the 1960s, most skaters wore very thin canvas shoes with a rubber sole, like the Converse All Star boots that were first launched back in 1917, though other brands soon entered this very promising new market.

Patti McGee on the cover of *LIFE* magazine, 1965.

A PIONEERING BRAND

The first Van Doren Rubber Company store opened its doors in California at the start of 1966, with its clientele rapidly rechristening it 'Vans'. It was the first brand designed by skaters for skaters and the iconic models it created have remained timeless to this day, making a deep impression on the collective imagination of the skating community.

The story began with the first model, Vans Authentic, which are still manufactured and sold today. Ten years later, in 1976, the skaters Tony Alva and Stacy Peralta gave their blessing to the Vans Era, which uniquely featured a padded collar. At the time, all the upper parts of the shoes were still being made from fabric, but in 1977 the first leather shoes were launched.

Vans Old Skools, instantly recognizable by their 'jazz stripe' (a white strip down the side that was essentially a simple scribble sketched by Paul Van Doren), appeared the same year, along with the lace-less Classic Slip-on. This was to become probably one of the brand's best-known models.

The invention of new skating tricks like the 'grip' and the 'ollie' in the 1980s put these shoes through their paces, however, and with the accumulated effect of the friction required to get the board to lift off, canvas shoes and thin shoes soon began to wear out.

Durability therefore became a crucial factor when choosing skating shoes, and as tricks evolved to scale even greater heights (literally) and with more and more rotations of the board, brands began to produce high-top boots reinforced with several thicknesses of material.

Vans Era shoes in their original blue/red scheme, designed by Tony Alva and Stacy Peralta.

© Division of Culture and the Arts, National Museum of American History, Smithsonian Institution

Vans also paved the way for many other shoe brands that were directly designed for skateboarding, notably Etnics (now known as Etnies), the first French brand. Their debut model was launched in 1986, followed (in 1987) by a second shoe featuring an image of Natas (full name, Natas Kaupas), a skating legend, the inventor of numerous 'slides' and a street skating pioneer.

This idea of a pro model was very much part of skateboarding culture – skaters could already buy a board featuring a picture of their idol. The first of these, featuring Natas, had been launched in 1980, and the following year Vans contacted Steve Caballero (a legendary skater, a member of the Bones Brigade and the inventor of the 'caballerial') to arrange a contract: the Vans Cab hit the market in 1989, styled on the since-discontinued Vans 138 and featuring Caballero's signature dragon motif that appeared on his pro model boards.

It's worth noting that the fashion for high-tops with lots of padding gradually faded in the 1990s, just when boards were beginning to shrink to provide more flexibility during rotations. A direct upshot of this development was that the criteria for choosing the right shoes began to change, since it's the freedom for movement in the ankle, essential for performing tricks, that is of paramount importance. Although Vans Cabs are still a popular choice for many skaters, their high-top shape poses a real problem and some skaters began cutting off the top of the upper part of the shoe before this trimmed-back shape was officially introduced by Vans in 1992 with the Half Cab.

The Vans Steve Caballero pro model, 1988.

French advertising campaign for the Natas pro model produced by the Etnies brand. >

NATAS
Notre Dame
NATAS
ETNIES

OR 'HOW SNEAKERS WERE APPROPRIATED'

At the time, the only affordable shoes that ticked all the boxes – durable high-tops with a reinforced toe box (the front part of the shoe) – were basketball sneakers, and Nike's leather Air Jordan 1s became very popular in the skating community, as did the brand's Dunk model. These had initially been designed for American university basketball teams and were launched in the 1980s. Finding little traction in the NBA (for comfort reasons), they were mostly shunned by professional basketball players in the 1980s–1990s and so could often be found discounted. This was all it took for skaters to hijack the model even as production was being wound down, at precisely the moment when skateboarding culture was booming and riders were turning to brands designed by them and for them, such as Etnies. Nike spotted this gap in the market and, in 1996, released the first three models exclusively dedicated to skateboarding, including the Nike SB Schimp, which marked the launch of the Nike SB offshoot brand. Nike even conducted a TV advertising campaign depicting skaters not as rebels but as athletes.

It was a commercial disaster – the pairing had nothing to say and was a flop with a community that at the time was searching for an identity. The lesson for the brand was not to try to launch a shoe from nothing but instead to build a legend on the pre-existing success of basketball boots like the Dunk. Nike SB then produced a reinforced Dunk, wholly in tune with the times and deliberately designed for skaters based on a model that had already proven its success. The Dunk SB was the hit shoe of the year in both fashion and skateboarding and spawned a series of collaborations, such as with the popular rapper Travis Scott, sparking further hype around the model for the rest of the year.

Skateboarding became an Olympic event in 2020 and to mark the occasion, Nike SB, which also makes kit for various teams, decided to work with Dutch artist and designer Piet Parra (a collaborator with the brand on several previous models, most notably the Air Max 1 of 2018). This collaboration led to the release of a new Dunk SB, the Low Parra, in line with the launch of a range of jerseys featuring graphics.

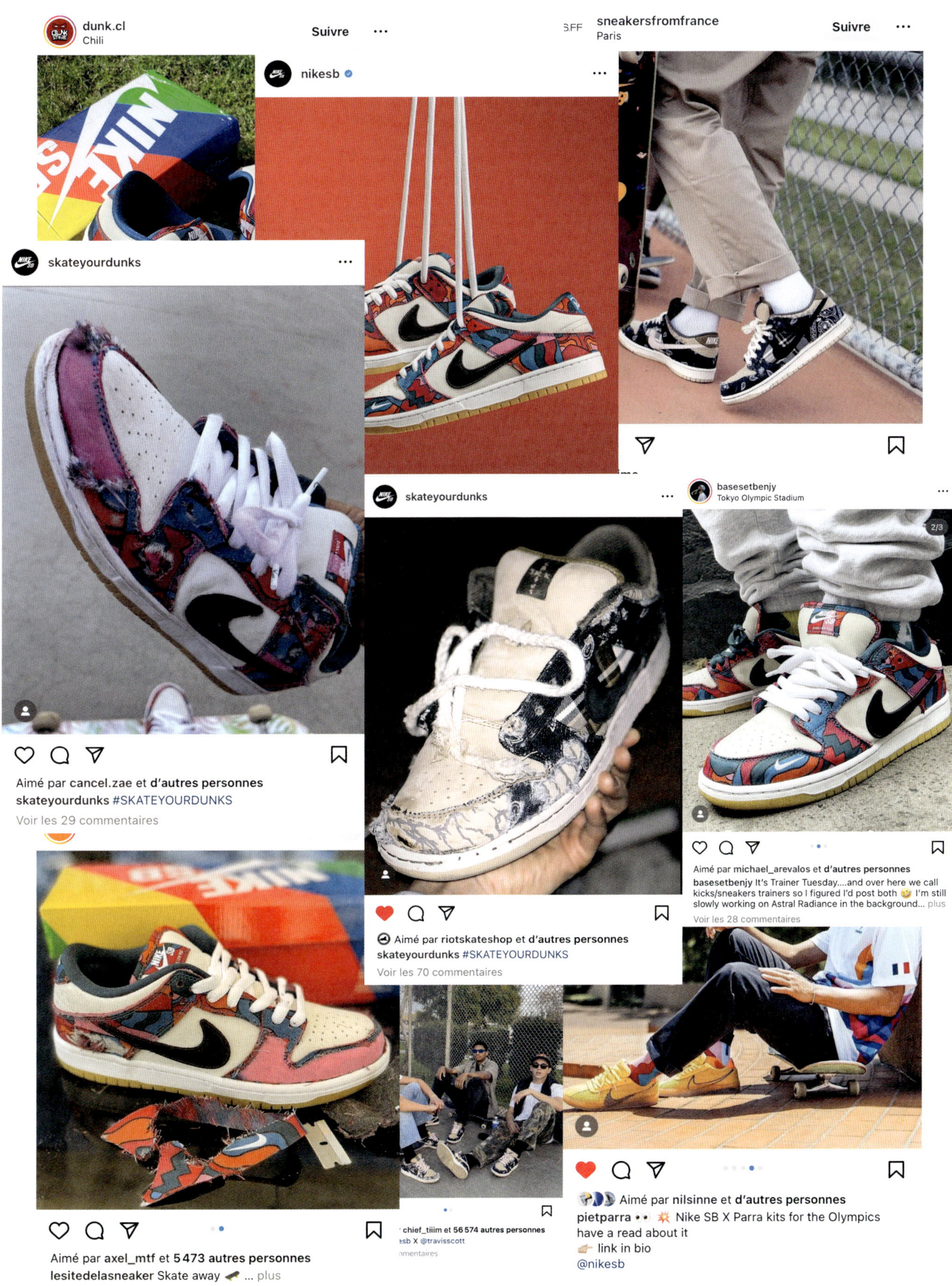
dunk.cl
Chili
Suivre
sneakersfromfrance
Paris
Suivre
nikesb
skateyourdunks
Aimé par cancel.zae et d'autres personnes
skateyourdunks #SKATEYOURDUNKS
Voir les 29 commentaires
skateyourdunks
Aimé par riotskateshop et d'autres personnes
skateyourdunks #SKATEYOURDUNKS
Voir les 70 commentaires
basesetbenjy
Tokyo Olympic Stadium
Aimé par michael_arevalos et d'autres personnes
basesetbenjy It's Trainer Tuesday....and over here we call kicks/sneakers trainers so I figured I'd post both I'm still slowly working on Astral Radiance in the background... plus
Voir les 28 commentaires
Aimé par axel_mtf et 5 473 autres personnes
lesitedelasneaker Skate away ... plus
Aimé par nilsinne et d'autres personnes
pietparra Nike SB X Parra kits for the Olympics
have a read about it
link in bio
@nikesb

ADIDAS

RIDING THE WAVE

In 1989, Adidas was undergoing major restructuring as it addressed a problem with the sale and marketing of its products. The brand (with its signature three stripes) needed to rejuvenate its image if it was to take advantage of the growing popularity of a sport that promised new markets. After several years of research and development, Adidas Skateboarding finally saw the light of day in 2006, initially in the form of collaborations with big names such as skater and artist Mark Gonzales, who has now become the face of the brand. By choosing Gonzales to represent the brand, Adidas hoped to integrate not only the sporting aspects of skateboarding as a discipline but also skateboarding as a whole culture and lifestyle.

Adidas Skateboarding was to release a number of different models over the years. The great comeback of B-Ball (basketball) boots in 2020–2021 also coincided with the return of the Superstar that had been launched in 1969, and the Forum 84 in the skateboarding section at the end of 2020 with the skateboarder Heitor Da Silva's pro model. The brand similarly revisited its Superstar in 2020 with a design by Mark Gonzales, who made use of the opportunity to reprise his little ghost motif for the occasion.

laterkader
Aimé par chief_tiiim et 126 126 autres person
laterkader Purp purp purp purp purp purp purp purp purppppppp
adidasskateboarding
route_one
Suivre
idasskateboarding
1/7
paradeworld
Suivre
vincent
Voir les
idasskateboarding
Suivi(
Aimé par yo_daiiii et 11 764 autres personnes
adidasskateboarding /// Mark Gonzales Switch Blunt in NYC, wearing the NORA signature model... plus
Aimé par notis_aggelis, desir_europe et 3 406 autres personnes
paradeworld @heitordasilva in the Forum 84' ADV... plus
r blabacphoto, blondey et 24 327 autres
kateboarding Introducing the Superstar by... plus
Aimé par jeffsuds et 17 182 autres personnes
adidasskateboarding /// マイテ・スティーンハウトがデザイ ンを手掛けたAdimatic Mid by Maité。 スエードを使用したマルチレイヤー構 造により、優れた耐久性を発... plus

OTHER BRANDS

By the late 1990s, shoes were becoming ever more sophisticated and they incorporated as much technology as possible, with air pockets in the soles, reinforced elements and loops for laces. All these features led to the creation of certain models that have become stars, such as the éS Koston 1 and the DVS.

Skateboarding shoe fashion has alternated between thick and thin shoes ever since, and the same is true of the trends in the cut and width of pants. However, within certain brands, some skaters with strong identities sometimes buck trends in skate shoes.

In 2014, the HUF brand launched a pro model for the legendary Dylan Rieder, one of the greats for many. Although he has achieved fame for his talent and his unique and classy style, not to mention his model good looks, Dylan made his mark here with a black-and-white video compilation of his tricks to a soundtrack of Sturgill Simpson, who has been a source of inspiration for many skaters. When HUF was looking to make a model for Dylan, he stipulated that it be suitable both for riding a board and an evening on the town. So HUF launched first a model with the look of a shoe that could be worn in the evening and then a second in the form of a moccasin. This look has been around ever since and can be found today in brands like Vans and Globe, with models such as the one created in collaboration with the *Wasted Talent* magazine and store.

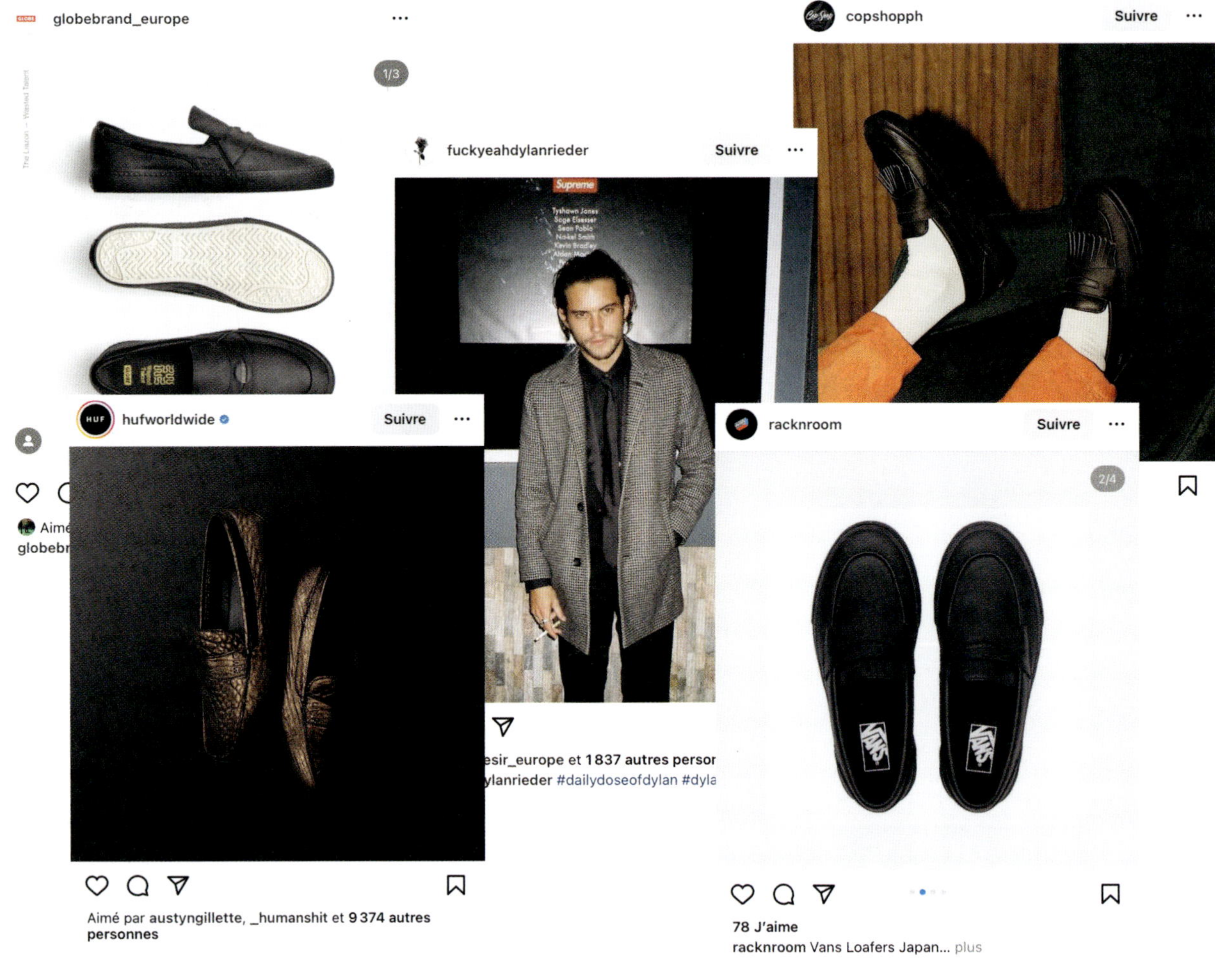

The éS Koston 1, first released in 1997. >

koston

Après les sportifs de toutes disciplines les vedettes ont pris goût au skate. Chaque mois nous vous offrirons un reportage sur vos chanteurs et comédiens préférés qui ont choisi la planche à roulettes. Nous ouvrons cette rubrique par des femmes : deux chanteuses, Rika Zaraï et Joëlle du groupe « Il était une fois », une comédienne, Anne Jolivet, qui fut la célèbre « Noëlle aux quatre vents » de la télévision. Toutes trois se sont pasionnées pour ce nouveau sport et l'ont adopté.

DU SHOW-BIZ SUR LES PLANCHES

AN ECOSYSTEM GOES MAINSTREAM

From the very early days, when skateboarding enthusiasts were making their own boards, to the recent interest shown by luxury brands and museums, skateboarding has always been capable of evolving and adapting to trends. It has spanned a number of different eras, from the first brands to embrace a hippy and surfer identity in the 1970s to the punk and rock references of the 1980s and 1990s.

< A page from the magazine *Skate France International* no. 3, The Geneva Skateboard Museum.
Photo © Nicolas Barthélémy

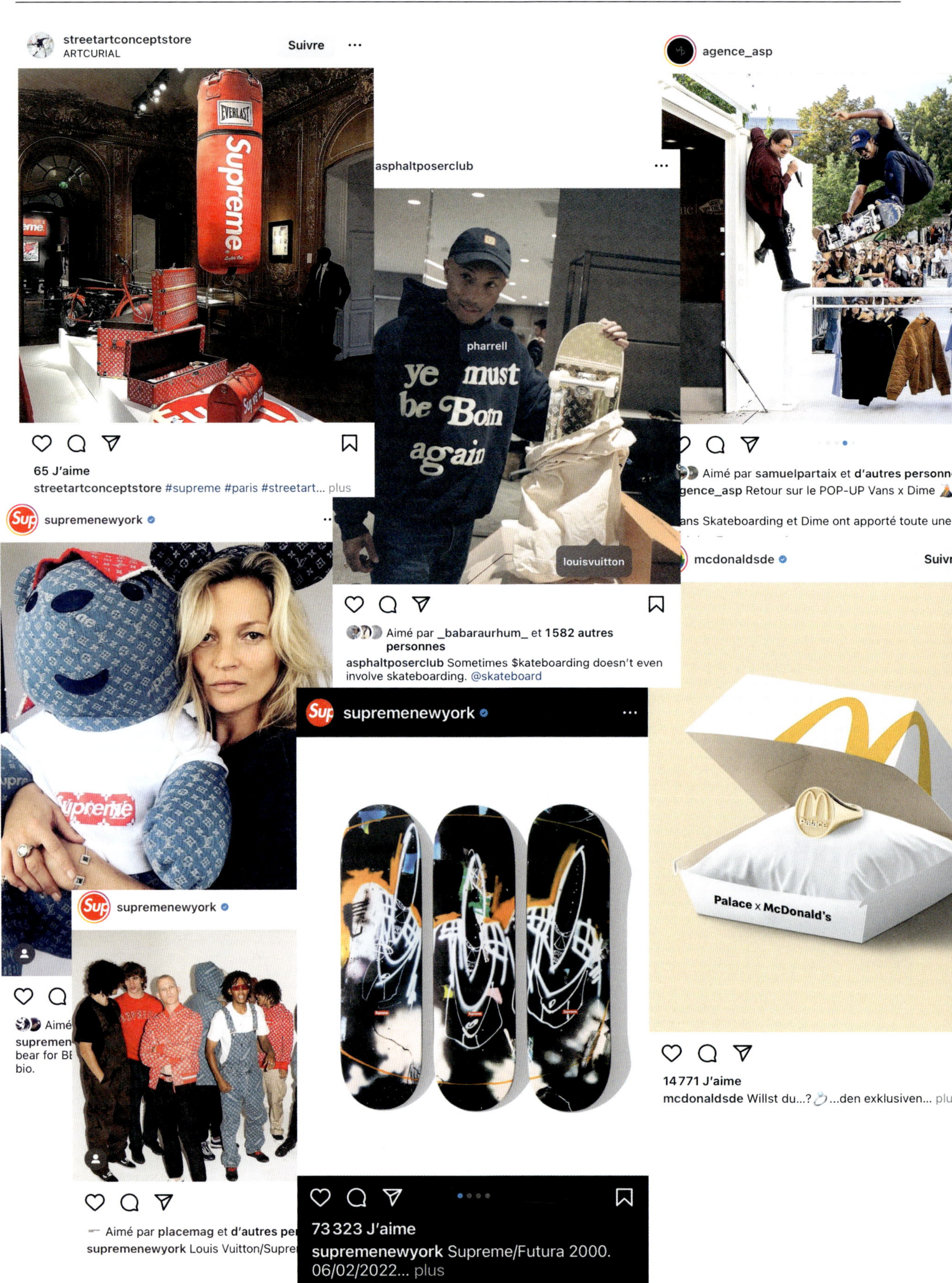
streetartconceptstore
ARTCURIAL
Suivre
EVERLAST
Supreme
65 J'aime
streetartconceptstore #supreme #paris #streetart... plus
asphaltposerclub
pharrell
ye must be Born again
louisvuitton
Aimé par _babaraurhum_ et 1582 autres personnes
asphaltposerclub Sometimes $kateboarding doesn't even involve skateboarding. @skateboard
agence_asp
Aimé par samuelpartaix et d'autres personnes
gence_asp Retour sur le POP-UP Vans x Dime
ans Skateboarding et Dime ont apporté toute une...
supremenewyork
Supreme
Aimé
supremen
bear for BE
bio.
supremenewyork
Aimé par placemag et d'autres per
supremenewyork Louis Vuitton/Supre
supremenewyork
73 323 J'aime
supremenewyork Supreme/Futura 2000.
06/02/2022... plus
mcdonaldsde
Suivre
Palace x McDonald's
14 771 J'aime
mcdonaldsde Willst du...? ...den exklusiven... plus

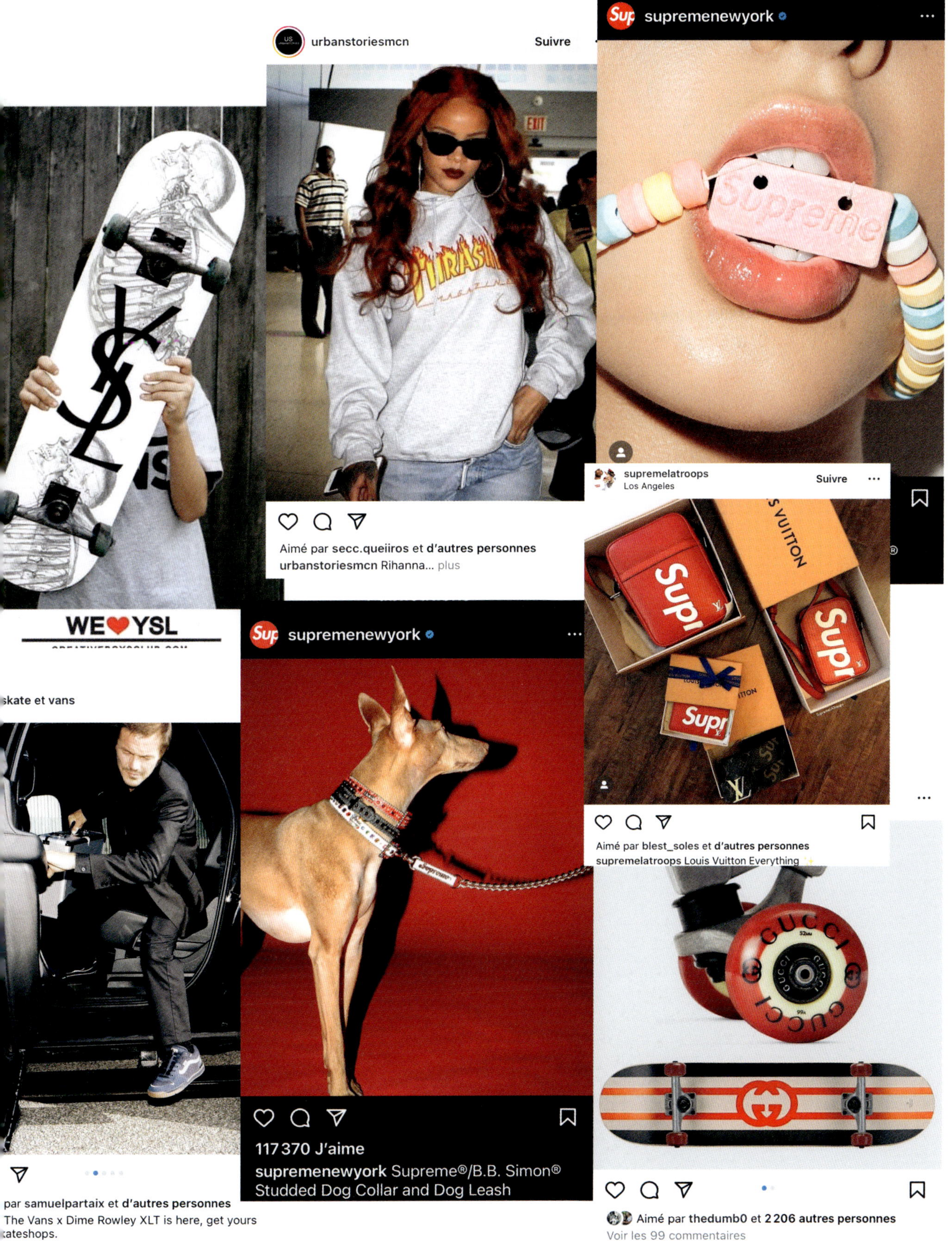
urbanstoriesmcn
Suivre
Aimé par secc.queiiros et d'autres personnes
urbanstoriesmcn Rihanna... plus
supremenewyork
supremelatroops
Los Angeles
Suivre
Aimé par blest_soles et d'autres personnes
supremelatroops Louis Vuitton Everything
WE ♥ YSL
skate et vans
supremenewyork
117 370 J'aime
supremenewyork Supreme®/B.B. Simon® Studded Dog Collar and Dog Leash
par samuelpartaix et d'autres personnes
The Vans x Dime Rowley XLT is here, get yours
ateshops.
Aimé par thedumb0 et 2 206 autres personnes
Voir les 99 commentaires

Skateboarding Barbie.
Photo © Nicolas Scordia

The first video clips soon began appearing on television, and meet-ups and competitions were also organized. At the same time, brands began to take an interest in sponsorship as they tried to find a way into skateboarding culture, and of belonging to the movement.

Brands that had initially had nothing to do with skateboarding then tried to associate their image with the sport to attract a new audience. This was especially true of Mattel with its skating Barbie doll, but many other toy manufacturers also tried to jump on the bandwagon. The Tech Deck, a miniature skateboard steered with the fingers, rapidly took off in schools, to the occasional consternation of teachers.

Children are a key market segment for the skateboarding industry, which has sometimes developed targeted designs that include cartoon characters such as Bart Simpson. In September 2023, the Santa Cruz brand launched a limited run of boards that were packaged randomly like collectible trading cards, recalling the Pokémon card craze of 1999.

A Tech Deck case.
Photo © Nicolas Scordia

The trends driven by skateboard brands have almost always evolved on the margins, highlighting the underground aspects of the movement, which has been a major selling point for the teenage audience targeted by industries of this kind. There is no escaping the lure of profit, however, and various influences have conspired to make the ecosystem a little more mainstream.

Collaborations between different brands have become increasingly common, making it possible to reach potential customers across two distinct artistic identities; the Quebec brand Dime joined forces with the giant Vans machine during Paris Fashion Week in 2023, and the Palace brand has collaborated on a more ad hoc basis with McDonald's fast food restaurants.

When celebrities such as Rihanna or Justin Bieber appeared on the cover of gossip magazines sporting the logo of the specialist magazine *Thrasher*, famous for its punk, even quite trashy, image, a whole generation of teenagers turned it into an essential fashion accessory. This caused a certain amount of disgruntlement among purists as they felt that an element of their culture had been appropriated by the uninitiated, who, according to some people, knew nothing of such magazines.

Despite a collaboration with the luxury brand Louis Vuitton in 2017, brands like Supreme have always tried to be choosy about their customers; when they opened their store in the Marais in Paris, you had to take part in a draw for a chance to go to the 'DROP' day (new product launch) during the week.

The world of skateboarding is essentially becoming ever more visible, whether in fashion, as partnerships with luxury brands proliferate, in sports, with, for example, admission to the Olympic Games, or in the cultural sphere, as various museums begin to take an interest.

A board entitled *Failed Experiments (Blue)* featuring the cartoon character Bart Simpson, reworked by the artist Alexander-John, 2021.
Photo © Nicolas Scordia

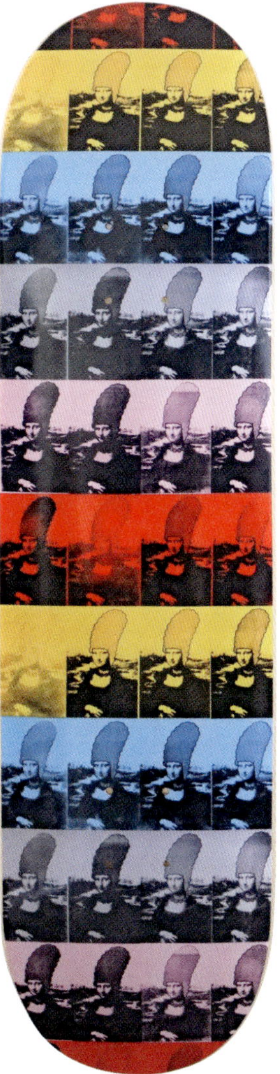

• (Top left) Board referencing the original logo of the Powell Peralta brand with a skull shaped like Homer Simpson.
The Geneva Skateboard Museum

• (Top right, centre left and bottom left) Santa Cruz X Pokémon and Santa Cruz X Marvel collections.
The Geneva Skateboard Museum/ photo © Leyla Madoeuf

• (Bottom right) Board entitled *Mona Simpson* featuring a design by the artist Nick Walker superimposing the facial features of Marge Simpson onto the Mona Lisa in a graphical style reminiscent of Andy Warhol.
Photo © Leyla Madoeuf

Vinyl copy of *Skateboard Baby* by Lady Skate and the Skateboard Kids, 1977.
© Nicolas Scordia

MUSIC AND MOVIES

THE ROAD TO GLOBAL RECOGNITION

Over the years, and as proof of the passion it inspires, skateboarding has outgrown its status as a sport or a simple hobby to become a real cultural phenomenon influencing many different aspects of popular culture, especially music and filmmaking.

THE SOUNDTRACK

As discussed, skateboarding was initially heavily dependent on the surf culture that was exploding at the time, and musically it was inseparable from the West Coast of the United States in the 1960s, where it all began for these sidewalk surfers.

Bands were starting to put skateboarding to music, faithfully reproducing the stylings of surf rock and artists such as the Beach Boys, who released their famous hit 'Surfin' USA' in 1963. Following Woodstock in 1969, the early 1970s were steeped in hippy ideology and psychedelic rock. The tone of the times was for global messages of peace, love and kindness.

Boards from the Zeropolis brand's *Club 27* series paying homage to (from left to right) Jim Morrison, Janis Joplin and Jimi Hendrix.
Photo © Leyla Madoeuf

Owen Nieder performing a layback air at the Del Mar Skate Ranch, 1980s. >
Photo © J. Grant Brittain

ARCADE

HUF X AC/DC board.
Photo © Leyla Madoeuf

Rock music exploded onto the world stage, a movement of young people that kept pace with the technological innovation of the times and grew principally in response to the desire of these new generations to rebel against the music and cultural references of their parents.

In total contrast to the optimistic and naïve messaging of the preceding decade, the 1980s were marked by the emergence of punk and hard rock.

Skateboarding was going through a rough patch at the time, as young people perceived it as being too closely associated with a past they saw as outdated. The birth of street skating and the proliferation of bans on skating in public spaces marked the first step towards a more subversive image that would of course appeal to a teenage audience in search of thrills and excitement.

A new and more urban genre of music – hip-hop – arrived in the 1990s, immediately attracting the attention of the skateboarding community, which rapidly became associated with this new genre. More than just a musical movement, hip-hop, which emerged in New York in 1973, encompassed four major disciplines: dance, rap (or 'MC-ing'), graffiti and DJ-ing.

A pop-punk movement surfaced at the turn of the 2000s with Avril Lavigne as its ambassador. The French-Canadian singer–songwriter has sold more than 50 million singles, including memorable cuts like *Complicated* and *Sk8er Boi*, both of which were released in 2002.

Board featuring a photo of an unidentified popper taken at the Roseland Ballroom, New York, by Joe Conzo, Jr.
Photo © Leyla Madoeuf

Element X Public Enemy boards.
Photo © Leyla Madoeuf

Natas Kaupas snapped wearing a Public Enemy T-shirt,1988. >
Photo © J. Grant Brittain

PUBLIC
ENEMY

Skateboarding has been constantly reinventing itself for some years, appropriating and popularizing new cultural contexts and backgrounds. A close look at the changes in the frames of reference used by the industry reveals a somewhat schizophrenic trend towards being both bankable and underground – as if, despite the strong economic imperatives of the market, there is still a desire to remain outside the mainstream and to culturally differentiate skaters from non-skaters.

Evidence of this has recently been provided by a renewed interest in jazz, with American brands like Supreme and HUF bringing out boards featuring Miles Davis and even clothing collections bearing the image of John Coltrane.

The French brand Magenta Skateboards from Bordeaux has made a concerted effort to forge a close link with classic jazz through both its boards and its videos.

HUF X Miles Davis board.
Photo © Leyla Madoeuf

>

Free Jazz series designed by Soy Panday for the Bordeaux brand Magenta.

From left to right, images of: Thelonious Monk; Ella Fitzgerald at her concert at New York's Downbeat jazz club in 1947; Chet Baker on stage in Amsterdam in 1983; Miles Davis on the sleeve of *Doo-Bop*, his hip-hop album; Django Reinhardt; a portrait of Art Blakey by Francis Wolff; Aretha Franklin live in Palermo; and Bill Evans in Copenhagen, photographed by Jan Persson.
© Soy Panday/Courtesy Magenta Skateboard

JAMEEL
Magenta
VIVIEN FEIL
Magenta
BEN GORE
Magenta
CASEY FOLEY
RUBEN SPELTA
Magenta
LEO VALLS
Magenta
JIMMY LANNON
Magenta
GLEN FOX
Magenta

Antiz boards featuring album sleeves altered to include the brand's signature typeface and graphics (such as an inverted 'A' or an owl).

Julien Bachelier, founder of the French brand Antiz from Lyon, has stated that music, and rock in particular, has been part and parcel of the brand's identity from the outset.

'We have remained in Lyon to this day, and have just moved district. Paul and Come (two young locals) are on hand to fold some T-shirts. The 13th Floor Elevators is on the sound system – they choose their playlist.

'It all takes me back to the beginnings of Antiz at the turn of the 2000s; Sathonay's apartment, roommates from all over Europe and posters for the Ground Zero concert plastered on the sitting room walls; music and skateboarding have always been two sides of the same coin. For many of us, the musical and visual culture of what makes a skater was developed from videos and magazines, and Antiz has allowed us to lay claim to the rock side of European skateboarding. We have been paying homage to our idols since the very first series – Misfits for Hugo, Hellacopters for Love, Roxy Music for Juju – and we have continued with album covers. Joy Division and the involvement of Peter Saville (artistic director for Joy Division and New Order among others) set the tone.

'The important thing was not subversion or being provocative; the focus has simply been on passing something on, sharing, listening and watching. All this was very naïve and wide-eyed – there was no plan B and, 20 years later, we are still here.'

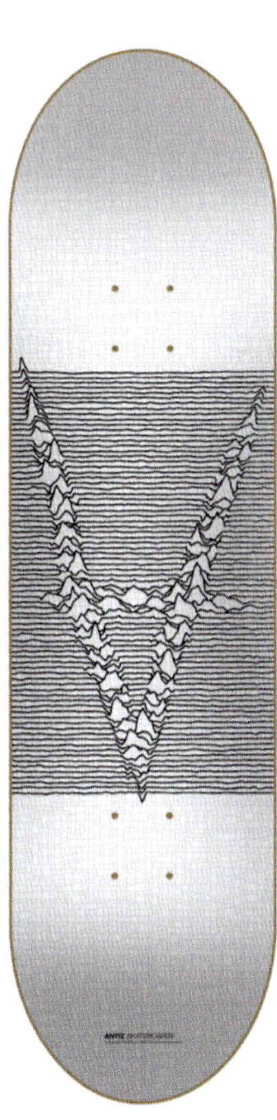

THE IMAGE BOARD

The accumulation (and appropriation) of cultural references was now an integral part of the graphic richness of 'skate art' and, as with music, videos and film references played a key role in this trend.

Video, which appeared in the 1980s, created a real revolution and was rapidly assimilated as a means of communication both by a group of skaters wishing to assert their own identity and by brands in search of new audiences. Music was never far away in either case.

Bones Brigade video cassettes.

Only ten years later, video cameras had become increasingly affordable and the volume of professional and amateur videos was soaring. This era is particularly associated with skateboarding, not least because video meant it was barely ever out of the media. It was also a time when graphic designers were allowing themselves more freedom to appropriate (and misappropriate) logos, intellectual property and album covers, and there was more than one way to reuse a cultural reference.

In one example, Antiz restyled the iconic *Jaws* poster for a pro model board for the French skater Robin Bolian. The image was unmistakable, except that the shark had been replaced by the brand's logo in a crude reworking of the famous image with no official collaboration with the copyright holders. This was not the case with Element, however, which recently collaborated with the Star Wars franchise to create several limited edition series of boards. The boards below feature designs created in the 1980s by the Santa Cruz graphic artist Jim Phillips for skateboarder Rob Roskopp that have been reinterpreted more recently for the launch of Season 4 of the Netflix series *Stranger Things*. The show has been a massive success, beating audience records with more than a billion hours of views, and the boards have been released as very limited editions. In addition to its importance as a cultural reference, the pattern on this limited edition board also changes depending on the angle from which it is viewed, an effect that makes it a unique and referential work of art.

Santa Cruz Rob Roskopp X *Stranger Things* boards with lenticular printing.
D.R.

Element X Star Wars & Santa Cruz X Star Wars boards; Princess Leia.
Photo © Leyla Madoeuf

STAR
WARS

The relationship between skateboarding and the movies was not limited to this kind of visual appropriation, however. Skateboarding has also featured in film as an essential plot element, with Marty McFly's cult hoverboard playing a key role in 1989's *Back to the Future Part II.* Skateboards have enjoyed increasing screen presence since the 2000s, such as in the plot constructed around a skatepark in Gus Van Sant's *Paranoid Park* of 2007 and the skateboarding communities that are the heroes of *We Are Blood*, a film made by Ty Evans in 2015. We'll take a look back at a few other productions...

WASSUP ROCKERS, directed by Larry Clark in 2005, follows a group of teenagers from Guatemala and San Salvador living in a poor district of Los Angeles that is riddled with violence. Instead of falling in with the hip-hop culture that predominates in the area, they wear tight pants, listen to punk rock and go skateboarding. Their daily challenge is to escape the violence of their surroundings.

LORDS OF DOGTOWN, directed by Catherine Hardwicke in 2005, is set in California and tells the story of a group of skaters in the Dogtown area of Santa Monica and the Los Angeles suburb of Venice in the mid-1970s. It follows the adventures of surfers Tony Alva, Stacy Peralta and Jay Adams who founded the Z-Boys after discovering urethane wheels, which brought about a revolution in skateboarding. The gang achieve notoriety and success but are forced to deal with both internal and external conflict that results in the departure of some of its members.

STREET DREAMS, directed by Chris Zamoscianyk in 2009, stars Paul Rodriguez as Derrick Cabrera, a promising skateboarder from Chicago who dreams of finding a sponsor and turning professional. Despite his obvious talent, Derrick is faced with opposition from his parents and friends who cannot understand his passion for something they feel has no future. Despite these obstacles, Derrick refuses to give up and strives to prove them all wrong.

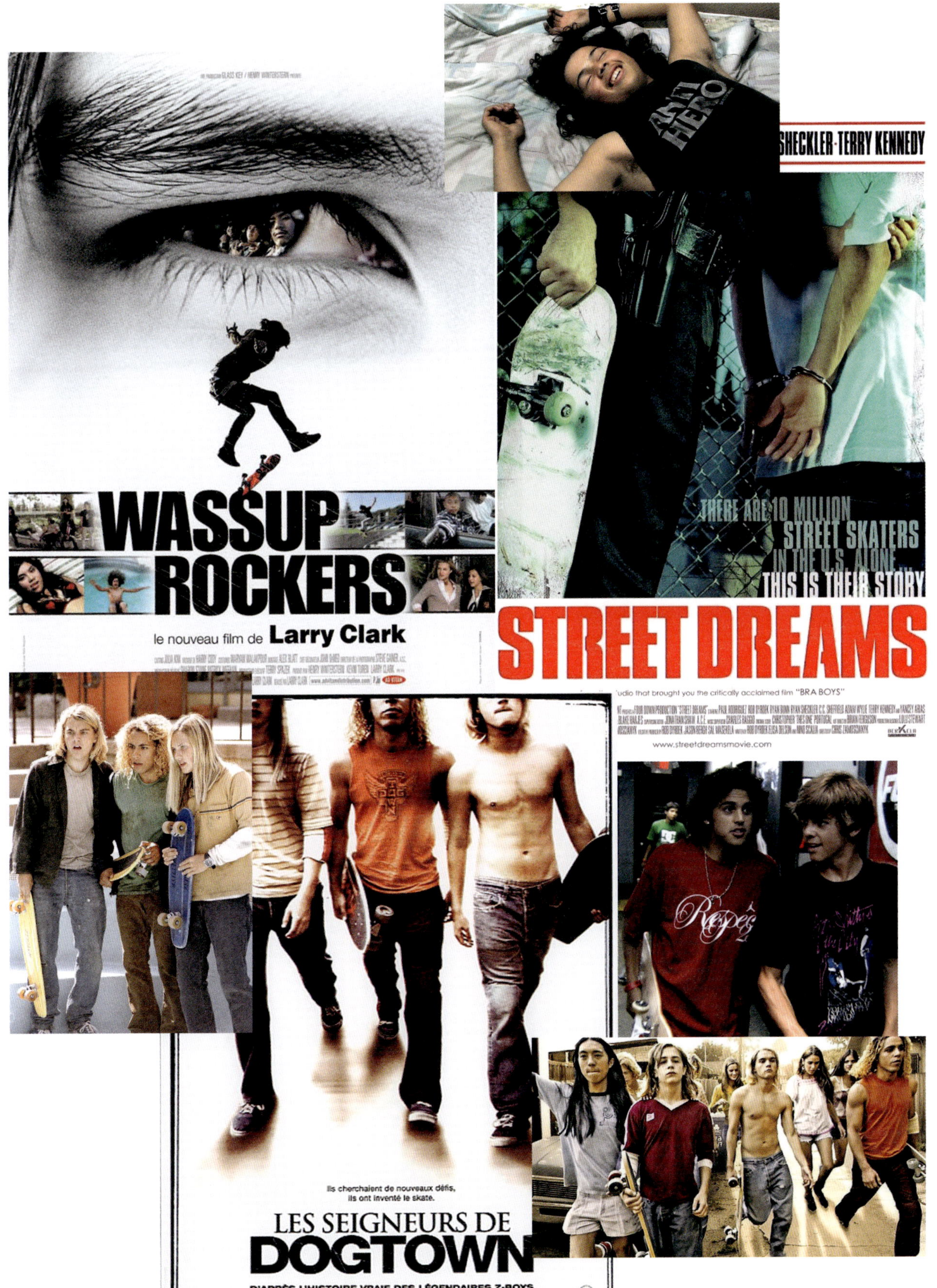

Posters and stills from the movies *Wassup Rockers, Street Dreams* and *Lords of Dogtown*.

Posters and stills taken from *Mid90s*, *Stay on Board* and *Bande de Skateuses*, a French documentary shot in 2021.

MID90S, directed by Jonah Hill in 2018, is set in Los Angeles and follows young Stevie, who is desperate to seem cool. Having tired of his Ninja Turtle bedding, cartoon T-shirts and TV nights in with his mother, Stevie develops a fascination for his older brother Ian's bedroom. He aspires to be just like Ian, even though his brother hits him regularly. Entering a local skateboarding store one day, Stevie is very taken with the fraternal spirit of a group of skating enthusiasts. He quickly acquires the nickname 'Sunburn' and manages to join the gang after passing several initiation tests.

STAY ON BOARD, directed by Nicola Marsh and Giovanni Reda in 2022, documents the life of legendary American skateboarder Leo Baker, who made it to the top despite the difficulties he encountered throughout his career as a transgender man. The film was released in 2022 and follows Baker and his teammates on the American national squad as they learn that skateboarding will feature as an Olympic sport for the first time at the Tokyo Games in 2020.

BANDE DE SKATEUSES ('Female skate gang') is a documentary directed by Marion Desquenne (2022) following pioneering Claire, who set up a forum for the first women skateboarders in France during the 2000s. It also features Shani Bru, the first female skateboarder to feature on the front cover of the French skate magazine *Sugar*, which seems like a seal of approval from the skating industry. In the documentary, the battle for the development of women's skateboarding in France is told through seven women over several generations, with a focus on strong values such as mutual aid.

SKATE FOR GOOD
SKATEBOARDING GETS INVOLVED

Skate for Good is an artistic and social movement that uses skateboarding as a vehicle for positive change and community development. It aims to promote inclusivity, education and social support by integrating skateboarding into initiatives to improve the lives of young people. Skateboarding is a hobby that transcends age, culture and origins, and the spaces in which it is enjoyed become places of learning, moral values and artistic expression – not to mention social cohesion.

Collaborative designed board entitled DK120, developed by the Decathlon Foundation to support the work of the Indian NGO Rural Changemakers.
Photo © Nicolas Scordia

A TOOL FOR INJECTING CHANGE

Organizations and community groups around the world are making use of skateboarding to drive beneficial change within their communities.

Over the last few years, skateboarding has become a popular platform for raising awareness of major issues such as environmental sustainability, social inclusion and justice. It is sometimes used as a quasi-educational tool to help young people feel connected and confident within their environment, or to raise funds for social causes.

One initiative example is the construction of skateparks in areas that do not have this type of infrastructure. These spaces provide a safe and accessible environment for local skaters while also strengthening community ties and promoting an active lifestyle. Big-name institutions such as the Tony Hawk Foundation and Skate Ghana have already carried out notable projects in this field.

In a parallel development, associations like the Decathlon Foundation have been supporting projects around the world in partnership with local organizations, NGOs and other enterprises, and it is important to point out that anyone can contribute to this movement, whether they are an influential VIP or a small business. Learn and Skate, which was founded in France by Jean Claude Geraud and Richard Schenten in 2012, is a good example.

One wall of the skatepark built by the Learn and Skate association in Mongolia (detail).
Photo © Martha Cooper

LEARN AND SKATE

The association's original aim was to promote skateboarding in deprived areas in order to give young people an opportunity to develop their skills. After it soon became clear that the hobby generated a real passion in the young people and contributed to them having a more fulfilling and productive life, however, the initial plan evolved to include the provision of new and second-hand equipment along with lessons for disadvantaged children.

Learn and Skate also raises funds to construct skateparks, schools and additional classrooms where these are required. In order to finance all these undertakings, it has organized exhibitions and sales of unique works created by famous urban artists. Other notable achievements include the creation of a new skatepark in Mukono in Uganda, which also has an educational element. The city of Kampala, the country's capital, has been the site of the oldest skatepark in East Africa since 2005. Their most recent project has been the construction of a skatepark in Ulaanbaatar, the capital of Mongolia. The foundation is striving to establish new partnerships to assure the sustainability of its undertakings and to extend these on a global scale.

Skatepark, Ulaanbaatar, Mongolia.
Photos © Martha Cooper

Skatepark, Ulaanbaatar, Mongolia. >

Photo © Martha Cooper

MULTIPLE INITIATIVES

In addition to building skateparks, many associations organize events and fundraisers online to support social causes such as education, mental health and humanitarian aid. Events take various forms, including meetings, competitions, auctions or gigs.

In some cases, it has been tragic losses such as that of the American professional skater and model Dylan Rieder, who died from cancer at a young age, that have left a deep impression on the worlds of skateboarding, music and fashion. The foundation that now bears his name raises funds by organizing events and through the support of socially involved brands such as Former, which donated in their entirety the profits generated by sales of a collection dedicated to the foundation.

One final inspiring story is that of Elaine Shallcross, an American who died of cancer at the age of 68 in 2020. Although never a skateboarder, she created an Instagram account and an online fundraising pool going by the name of *Shuvit Cancer*. To raise awareness of her initiative and to collect as much money as possible, she used the account to recount her progress in learning how to *shuvit*, a skateboard trick. Her Instagram account now has nearly 65,000 subscribers and the hashtag #shuvitcancer has been used in more than 10,000 posts.

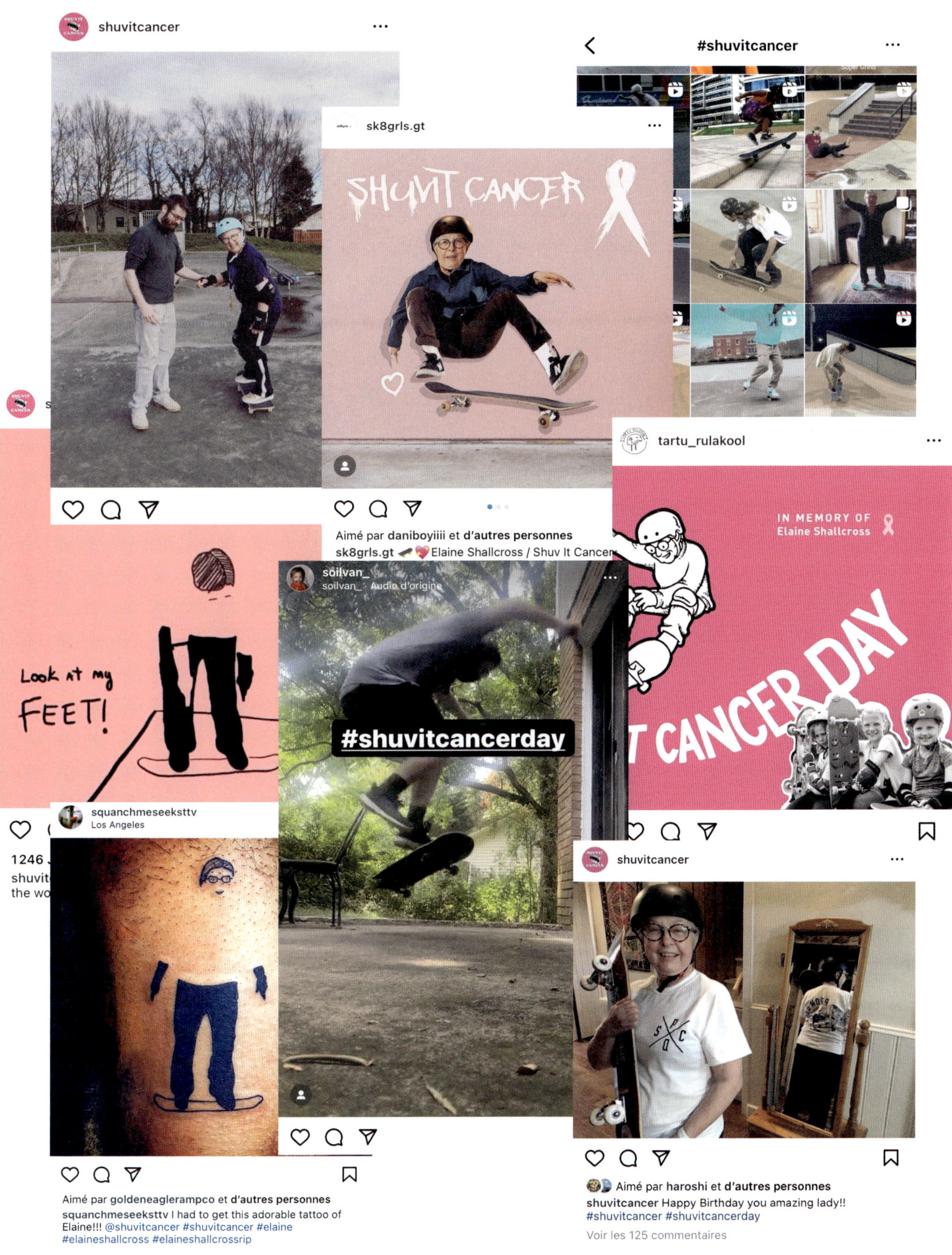
shuvitcancer
#shuvitcancer
sk8grls.gt
SHUVIT CANCER
Aimé par daniboyiiii et d'autres personnes
sk8grls.gt Elaine Shallcross / Shuv It Cancer
tartu_rulakool
IN MEMORY OF
Elaine Shallcross
T CANCER DAY
Look at my
FEET!
soilvan_
soilvan_ · Audio d'origine
#shuvitcancerday
squanchmeseeksttv
Los Angeles
Aimé par goldeneaglerampco et d'autres personnes
squanchmeseeksttv I had to get this adorable tattoo of Elaine!!! @shuvitcancer #shuvitcancer #elaine #elaineshallcross #elaineshallcrossrip
shuvitcancer
Aimé par haroshi et d'autres personnes
shuvitcancer Happy Birthday you amazing lady!! #shuvitcancer #shuvitcancerday
Voir les 125 commentaires

SEEING AND BEING SEEN

Skatepark in Tenerife, Canary Islands, painted by the Spanish artist Iker Muro.
Photo @ murone

SKATE SPOTS, SKATEPARKS AND DEMONSTRATIONS

Far from being a solitary practice, the skateboarding experience is shared with other people in the spaces where devotees congregate, and where sometimes wild, improvised exchanges and interactions occur. Skateboarding has found its niche within institutions and festivals, however, and images captured over decades of documentation have established it as an institution in its own right with its own particular style. Photographers and videographers capture every detail relating to the identity of skateboarding.

With tens of millions of enthusiasts worldwide, any attempt at being exhaustive would naturally be impossible, but we have chosen to focus on several places that we consider particularly relevant. It was difficult to choose, and we compared our experiences and encounters with skaters and discussed the impact such places had on skateboarding culture, along with their artistic interest.

Rather than being restricted by increasingly elaborate tricks, materials and streetwear, the history and sustainability of the sport has been underpinned by the interaction of its fans. Skateparks and similar spaces occupy a central place in the lives of skaters, wherever in the world they are found. This is where it all happens. People learn, teach and sympathize; they chart their progress and console each other after a fall.

In addition, growing numbers of events allow absolute beginners to discover skateboarding and old hands to share their passion by getting together and breathing new life into the culture.

While skateparks are places exclusively dedicated to sports like skateboarding, freestyle scootering and BMX, 'skate spots' are improvised places in which it is possible to skate; a simple bench or flight of steps in the street suffices, and these are known as 'street spots', although this term is also used for a place or a run that has been specially constructed.

Over the years, the lack of specific infrastructure has prompted skaters to build spots themselves, although this recourse to DIY is not just a last-ditch solution, instead echoing the spirit of research, creativity and adaptation that characterizes street skateboarding. A simple concrete connection across a patch of ground, an inclined plane to create a ramp, making an entire skatepark from virtually nothing – the possibilities are endless. These DIY locations are often built in secret and hushed up before ultimately being discovered and destroyed, although some have really established themselves definitively.

DIY construction of a park in Stuttgart, Germany, with David Eberle and Max Schröer shovelling wet concrete, 2022.
Photo © Matu Ostoja

First day of pouring concrete after postponement of demolition was announced by city hall.

The ramps are wrapped during construction to maintain a temperature that makes working with concrete easier.

Once the ramps have been finished, the 'flat' sections can be poured.

This part of the DIY build has been finished.
Photos © Matu Ostoja

< Laying the foundations of the DIY build in Stuttgart with David Höschele and Robin Wulf, 2023.
Photo © Matu Ostoja

Skateboarding in Paris has mostly been street skating; the idea has always been to find a place and adapt to its particular characteristics, which by their very nature are those parts of urban architecture most likely to provide opportunities for self-expression and competitive creativity. The French capital boasts many legendary street spots.

Le Dôme
Photo © Sylvie Barco

LE DÔME – PARIS – FRANCE

This is the name given by skaters to the space squeezed in between the Palais de Tokyo and the City of Paris Museum of Modern Art, which has become the historic symbol of skateboarding in Paris. The jumble of steps and curbs here has been skated by the greatest exponents of the art, and Le Dôme also features in the video game *Skater XL*. This is a place of pilgrimage for every skateboarder, amateur or professional.

THE PLACE DE LA RÉPUBLIQUE – PARIS – FRANCE

Skateboarding has historically always been tolerated here. The square has undergone several refurbishments, such as the installation of a 'multifunction skate/sit object' at its heart, bearing the logo of the Volcom brand, which has integrated itself seamlessly into the urban architecture, along with a 'manual pad' (a raised edge rather like a step or a sidewalk on which it is possible to do tricks on two wheels called 'manuals').

Elsa Garcia Despaigne performing a 'nose manual' in the Place de la République, Paris, 2023.
Photo © Jeff 'Suds' Sudmeier

Paul Brackett in the middle of a 'backside ollie' in the Place de la République, Paris, 2023. >
Photo © Jeff 'Suds' Sudmeier

PLACE DE LA BASTILLE – PARIS – FRANCE

This is a skate spot with plenty of skating modules. There is a permanent DIY concrete ramp and a marble curb, and numerous skate meets take place here every year, encouraging the construction of new obstacles.

Go Skateboarding Day event, Place de la Bastille, Paris, 2023.
D.R.

The women's skateboarding association Realaxe, founded in 2014 with the aim of providing weekly classes along with leisure activities and cultural events to bring together a community of women, has organized a number of mixers on the Place de la Bastille. The idea is to help female skaters to meet up, with events such as 'Queen of the Road', an idea borrowed from a day of the 'King of the Road' video programme created by magazine the American *Thrasher*. Teams of skaters compete in all kinds of challenges, with the winners being the team who win the most events. Each team is followed by a filmmaker whose job it is to make a recap video at the end.

'There are more and more girls at skateparks, but some are still having difficulties in finding their feet and asserting themselves,' says Sophie, the association president. She continues, 'We strive to create an inclusive atmosphere in which absolute beginners and the most experienced skaters are encouraged to get started, and this begins with skating together in an environment where everyone can feel at ease, whatever their skill level.'

In addition to these unmissable events, the city boasts several street spots that have achieved global fame. In August 2021, Red Bull even organized an event at the Trocadéro that brought together all the best skaters in the world to compete in a park where seven legendary spots had been recreated: the ledges of the Place de la République, the 'Bercy 5', the 'curb du Luxembourg' (a curved ledge), the wave sculpture at Châtelet, the 'melting house' at the Gare du Nord, the banks of the Seine and the Embâcle fountain on Place du Québec.

Session organized by the Realaxe association at the Bastille.
Photos © Renaud Marion

Hangar Darwin.
Photo © Bastien Maurence

LES CHARTRONS AND HANGAR DARWIN – BORDEAUX – FRANCE

The skatepark in the Chartrons district of Bordeaux (itself a UNESCO World Heritage site) is considered by some to be one of the finest in France. This exceptional space nestled on the quays alongside the Garonne river first opened in 2006 and incorporated two areas dedicated to street and park skateboarding.

After an initial renovation in 2011, it underwent further refurbishment (completed in 2022), which turned 25,565 square feet (2,375 square metres) of space into one of the largest street spots in the country.

It is now dedicated to street skateboarding and offers skaters the opportunity to express their passion and creativity on curbs, ledges, handrails and stairs. There is also a beginners' bowl.

Some relics from the past (such as the structure of the old bowl) have been given a new lease of life by the Hangar Darwin association.

Hangar Darwin.
Photo © Robin Briard and Bastien Maurence

Guilhem Mercadal, 2021.
Photo © Harvey Brepson

CITY HALL – LYON – FRANCE

The square at Place Louis-Pradel behind the City Hall is ideally located in the heart of Lyon and has acquired an international reputation as the world's best professional skaters come here to hone their skills. Local enthusiasts have also helped to make it a mecca for skateboarders by organizing a host of events such as the Slappy Challenge. Lyon has made its mark on the world of skateboarding even without a real skatepark worthy of the name. This spot was almost lost a few years ago but has been preserved thanks to an online petition that attracted more than 12,000 signatures. Through the dedication of fans like the photographer and videographer Fred Mortagne and the magic of the City Hall spot, Lyon has become an essential destination for world skateboarding, attracting skaters in search of new challenges and inspiration.

Estime Team at the skatepark in Saint-Jean-de-Maurienne.
© Yahel Galtier for Maison Shirak

SAINT-JEAN-DE-MAURIENNE – FRANCE

This skatepark in southeast France opened in 2017 as an initiative of the Skate and Create association and was built entirely by volunteers. It remains France's largest DIY construction project for skaters.

It is also an open-air museum that showcases artists like the Art by Friends collective who, in 2018, painted the handle of the enormous Opinel knife (which is 20ft/6m high, including 7ft/2.2m for the blade) that looms over the skatepark. You will also find graffiti of skaters by local artist Maurizio Galloro behind a section known as The Gates of Hell.

La Source, 1856,
by Jean-Auguste-Dominique Ingres,
1780–1867. Musée d'Orsay.

MONTAUBAN – FRANCE – BY CYRILLE GOUYETTE

Hollows and bumps, lines that follow curves or ignore them, flat areas that curve away and force a line: Marie Sforzini and Clément Merlin have created an artwork of contrasts that plays with the morphology of the skatepark to create a concave facsimile of the young woman painted by Ingres in his oil painting on canvas *La Source* ('The Spring'). The Old Master's painting has something sculptural, even mineral, about it, and plays with perspective, inviting us to imagine his model as a marble sculpture enclosed in a niche.

His 21st-century emulators have been more synthetic, creating a multi-layered geometric arrangement, a sort of bas-relief that you have to stroll around in order to properly appreciate its composition. Its Ingres-style silhouette is easily recognizable, outlining the female form with a raised right arm holding the base of a jug while the left supports it at the collar. We can also spot the *contrapposto* caused by the tilting of the shoulders under the weight of the jug and the swing of the hips in the opposite direction in response. Beyond this minimalist silhouette, however, the artists synthesize the figure by fragmenting it into disks that in places refer to the curves of the female form while elsewhere it frees itself from them.

The skater's journey is therefore structured through the provision of so many features for executing tricks. The artists also take an aquatic turn, preferring shades of blue and green over the original palette, and the disks are suddenly transformed into bubbles. However, the duo also use this homage to the Neoclassical master (who was born in Montauban) to magnify the linear outline that is its signature; by turns white and dark, the line is clear and precise, tracing the contours and reminding us that, for Ingres, draftsmanship was of primary importance when constructing a model. Here, the lines constitute both paths to follow and limits to exceed, inviting skaters to perform their most virtuoso tricks in this space and, in so doing, to create, in their turn, a three-dimensional work of art.

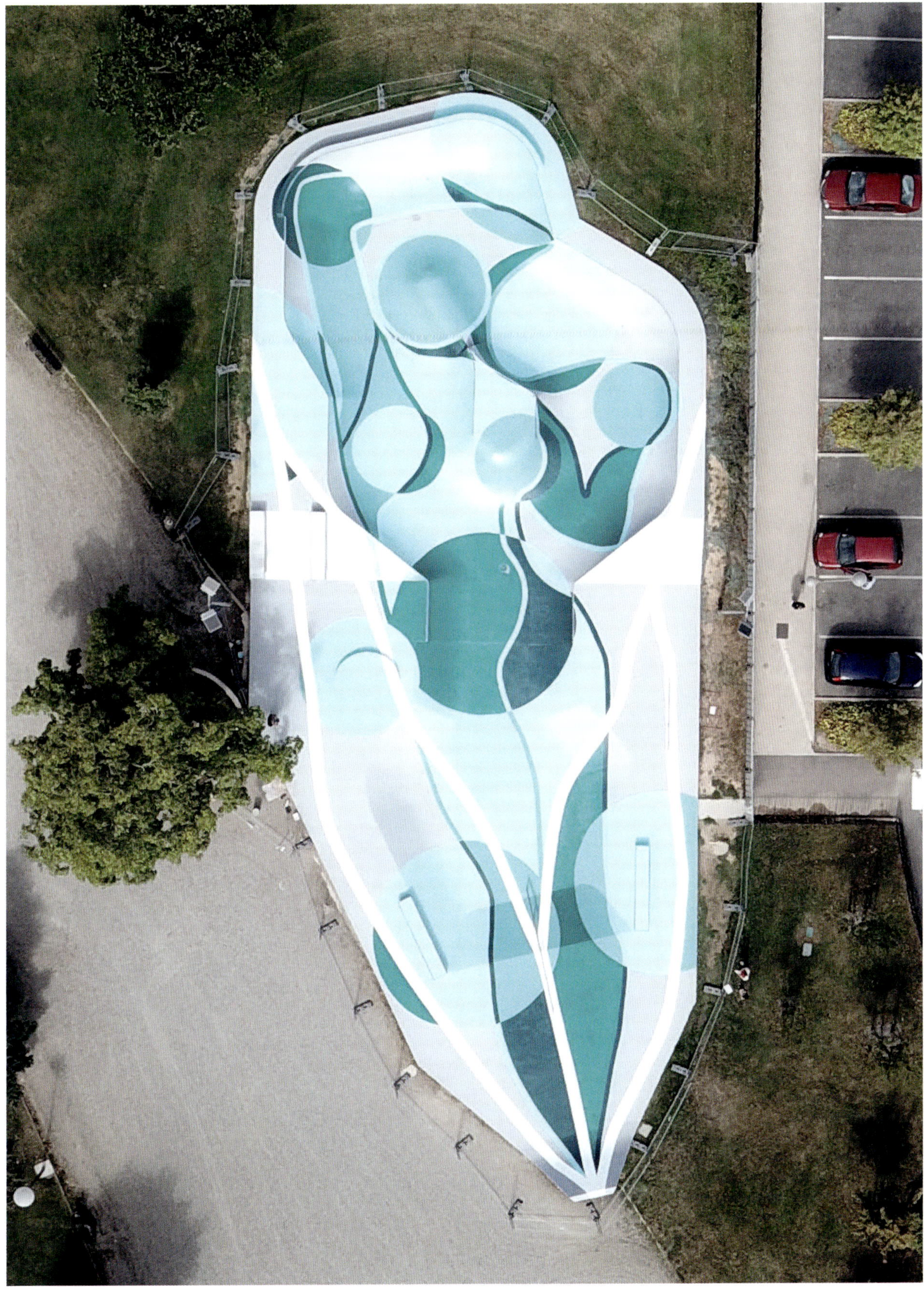

Montauban skatepark seen from a drone.
Photo © Marie & Clément

Chloé Bernard painting the Prado bowl in Marseilles, 2022.
Photo © Kevin Deschamp

THE PRADO BOWL – MARSEILLES – FRANCE

The Prado skate bowl (also known as the Bowl of Marseilles) opened in 1991 and is generally acknowledged to be the first concrete skatepark built in France. This perfect copy of the bowl at Huntington Beach in California is also located beside the sea and now plays host to international competitions such as the Quiksilver Bowlrider and the Red Bull Bowl Rippers. Artists are regularly commissioned to decorate its surface and the painter Chloé Bernard was a recent contributor.

Prado skate bowl, 2022. >
Photo © Chloé Bernard

Chloé Bernard at Cherbourg skate bowl.
D.R.

Chloé Bernard is a multidisciplinary artist based in Marseilles, with a residency at the Couvent Levat arts complex, who takes her inspiration from a surreal and nostalgic aesthetic. All her creations (and it is certainly the case here) feature vibrantly shaded worlds that transport those who experience them into strange dimensions. Her approach to painting skateparks is designed to highlight the 'hips', 'flats' and 'copings' in order to echo the architecture. Some of her creations also incorporate graphical elements taken from more traditional sporting infrastructure.

Chloé Bernard. >
Photo © Sarah Emma Smith

CRUZADE
SKATEBOARDS

Looking beyond the scene in France, European skating boasts a variety of equally important places for enthusiasts to meet, and we have selected two spots that we consider absolutely essential: the MACBA Museum of Contemporary Art of Barcelona, where art and skateboarding blend in a square with a unique atmosphere thanks to a fresco incorporating Keith Haring motifs; and the South Bank in London, a shrine to skateboarding in the heart of historic Britain.

MACBA – BARCELONA – SPAIN

Much like Le Dôme in Paris, the MACBA (Museum of Contemporary Art of Barcelona) is one of the most popular places with skaters from all over the world. Initially gaining fame on the scene for its four-block gap, the spot is now decorated with a reproduction of a fresco by Keith Haring.

In 1989, the New Yorker visited the Raval district of Barcelona (the current location of the MACBA) to paint at no charge a piece addressing the struggle with AIDS, a personal challenge that had greatly influenced his work. Twenty-five years later, the original painting, which was located on a dilapidated wall, was found to be in too poor a condition to be conserved and the museum authorities decided to make an identical reproduction at the rear of the building.

The fresco is now an essential part of any image of skaters at the MACBA, reinforcing the already existing links between this street artist and the world of skateboarding. The spot also symbolizes a certain state of mind, however, and as every element has become world famous, it is now a rite of passage for every fan of the sport. MACBA has also given its name to a media outlet that documents life and events at the spot, not to mention the eponymous skate store.

Mardel performing a switch flip at MACBA, 2023. >

Photo © Gabriel Renault

JUNTOS PODEMOS
PARAR EL SIDA

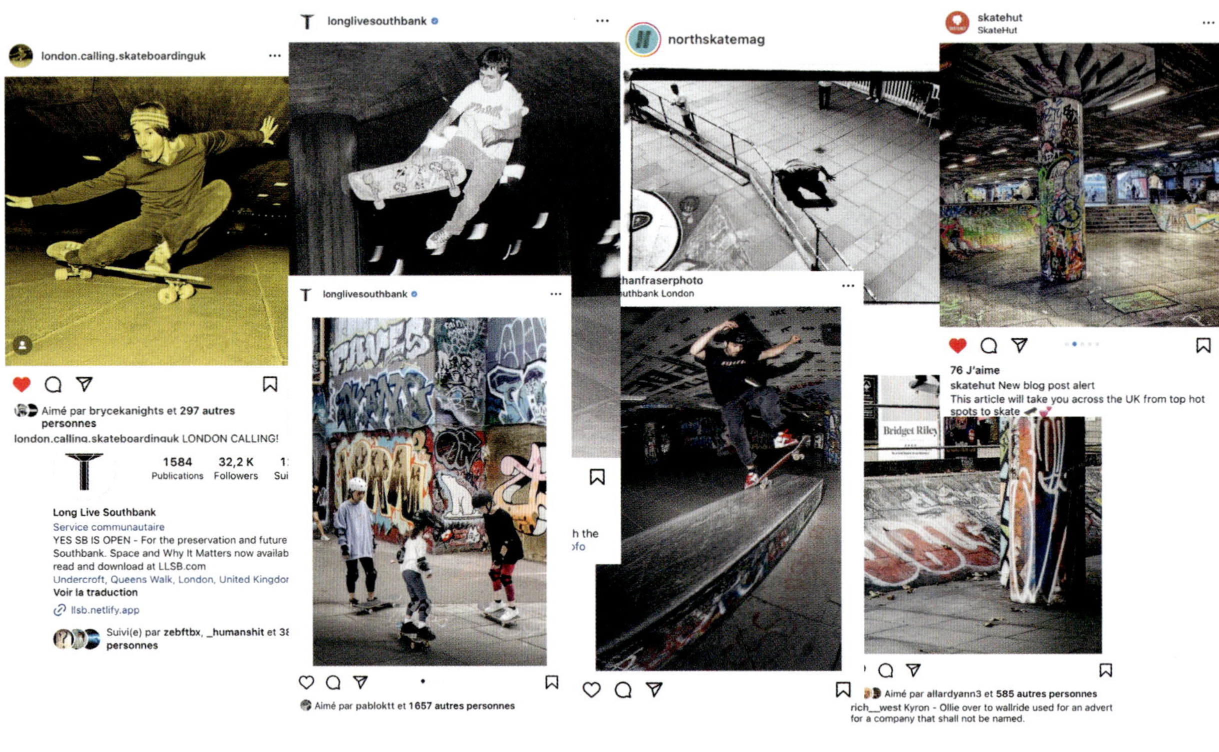

SOUTH BANK – LONDON – UNITED KINGDOM

The capital can be justly proud of the South Bank, an iconic and famous spot that is appreciated and beloved around the world. It was not just the birthplace of British skateboarding in the 1970s, but also a focal point for graffiti culture in London.

The undercroft of the Southbank Centre, which was to lend its name to the skatepark, is located on the banks of the Thames not far from the Tate Modern art gallery. It has become a shrine and a breeding-ground for skaters and street artists, and it all started because of the architecture of the place. It boasted both a ceiling and a smooth floor made up of inclined planes, and skaters made it their own in the 1970s in response to the assault on verticality that was going on at the same time in California. This underground space quickly became a rallying point for other activities such as street dancers, musicians and graffiti artists, and the Southbank Skate Space was to evolve as different worlds collided, creating over many years a true cultural heritage that was to spread throughout the world, featuring heavily in skating videos and magazines.

The spot, initially used in secret, became a proper skatepark in its own right. A melting pot of various sporting and artistic feats, it was recognized by the British Department for Digital, Culture, Media and Sport in 2012 although the whole South Bank area, along with the skatepark, was threatened with redevelopment only a year later. Thanks to the triumphant efforts of the Long Live Southbank campaign that was launched to save the space, it has remained an active site for skaters from the United Kingdom and artists who have taken up the mantle of previous generations.

Denver Adams performing a fakie flip, South Bank, 2021. >
Photo © Chris Dale

Rio de Janeiro, Brazil.

Chicago, United States.

Las Vegas, United States.

Goa, India.

Lisbon, Portugal.

Rio de Janeiro, Brazil.

Tel Aviv, Israel.

Goa, India.

Chicago, United States.

New York, United States.

Rio de Janeiro, Brazil.

Las Vegas, United States.

Tel Aviv, Israel.

Goa, India.

Cullera, Spain.

Rio de Janeiro, Brazil.

EXHIBITIONS AND FESTIVALS: FROM THE STREETS TO THE MUSEUM

Growing handplants skateboard, designed by Ryan McGinness.
Photo © Nicolas Scordia

Explanatory plaque in the form of a skateboard, also designed by Ryan McGinness for the Art Basel Miami, 2007.
Photo © Nicolas Scordia

Conveying a cultural phenomenon born in the streets into an exhibition does not seem like an obvious step on the face of it, but the art world experienced a new enthusiasm for urban culture and protest movements at the turn of the 2000s. A shift in understanding also took place among the museums, and these institutions slowly began to open their doors, creating an opportunity for skateboarding to invite itself in.

Quadriptych created by the GX1000 brand in collaboration with the photographer Dave Schubert and the artist Barry McGee.
D.R.

BEAUTIFUL LOSERS

This exhibition held at the Contemporary Arts Center (Cincinnati, Ohio) in 2004 brought together a collection of artists who went on to make history by creating a milestone in the approach to counter-cultures in the United States. This pioneering show in the world of street art even featured several skateboards as exhibits.

Some of the creative talents and artists from these urban and protest movements (such as graffiti artists) were still emerging at the time but had a passion for skateboarding. In Beautiful Losers they created an exhibition whose presentation of skateboards shook up the image of skateboarding by depicting it as an art form in its own right, influencing not only the way skaters saw themselves but also the way the general public perceived their culture.

The exhibitions were documented in a film directed by Aaron Rose in 2008, and a book featuring artists such as Shepard Fairey, Kaws, Barry McGee, Ryan McGinness and Margaret Kilgallen.

It is interesting to note that most of these artists and performers have now carved out a niche for themselves and achieved true recognition in the art world.

Since its creation, Beautiful Losers has been showcased in more than ten countries around the world and the exhibitions are now recognized to have cleared a path for wider acceptance and understanding of certain aspects of skateboarding culture as forms of cultural expressions.

Part of the magazine collection at The Geneva Skateboard Museum.
Photo © Nicolas Barthélémy

THE GENEVA SKATEBOARD MUSEUM – GENEVA – SWITZERLAND

This museum is of a size unique in Europe and was designed by Jim Zbinden, a former skater and the museum's current director. The project was piloted in 1995 with the creation of the Pulp68 brand and fully launched in the mid-2000s with the aims of promoting skateboarding, helping skaters and preserving and sharing its heritage. There are more than 1,500 skateboards and 25,000 objects (textiles, magazines, VHS recordings, shoes and stickers, etc.) on display. Pulp68 now releases special editions that are on view in the museum and one of the key pieces is a work by the Japanese artist Haroshi made from recycled skateboards. This is a place in which to experience and discover, but is also intended to be a creative workshop for local schools and a rite of passage for skating lessons and sessions for absolute beginners.

Jim Zbinden recommends watching the movies *Mid90s* (released in 2018) and *The End*, and taking a look at *Plaza*, which showcases the young people of Geneva and their talents. Jim's encyclopedic knowledge of skateboarding and the local scene makes this place an absolute must for anyone who is even remotely interested in the sport.

The Geneva Skateboard Museum.
Photo © Nicolas Barthélémy

ART OF SKATE – FLUCTUART, PARIS – 2022

In 2022, floating Parisian art centre Fluctuart hosted the *Art of Skate* exhibition, which presented an overview of the urban skateboarding scene.

In excess of 50,000 visitors had the opportunity to view more than 120 boards, along with 100 skate-related items by 80 artists from every corner of the world, including photos, posters, original artwork, sneakers, flyers and other objects connected with skateboarding culture, along with audio/video content, all curated around several themes.

More than 2,150 square feet (200 square metres) of exhibition space was devoted to showing how narrative writers, photographers, musicians, videographers and even brands (via collaborations) have engaged with the culture, and installations by Joachim Romain and the photographer and videographer Sylvie Barco were set up in situ. Following a chronological introduction, the exhibits covered various themes (Famous Writers, Skate for Everyone, Skate & Music, and so on) as well as the skate scene in France and the USA and the commitment of the artists, skaters and brands to humanitarian causes. The retrospective was rounded off with a look at skateboarding for young people and its recent adoption as an Olympic sport in Tokyo.

Exhibition *Art of Skate* at Fluctuart, Paris, 2022.
Photo © Sylvie Barco

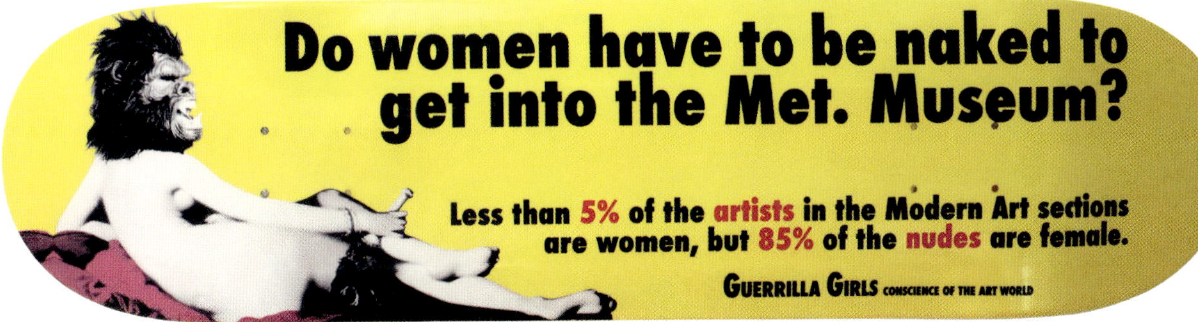

This Guerrilla Girls board, produced in partnership with Beyond the Street and exhibited at the *Art of Skate* exhibition, features one of the iconic posters produced by this group of feminist artists in the mid-1980s.
Photo © Leyla Madoeuf

JOACHIM ROMAIN

The artist contributed an immersive fresco to the exhibition that included well-worn and battered Californian boards. The installation also featured posters from around skateparks. In his work *Hate is Over*, the artist illustrated the goodwill and willingness to emulate others that are found among skaters, whatever their level of technical skill.

Lacadur skateboard featuring work by the artist Joachim Romain for the exhibition in 2022.

A close-up of part of Joachim Romain's fresco, 2022. >

GANG OF SKATE
GRIMPLE STIX

ËRELL

Ërell is a Paris-based street artist with a background in the world of graffiti. He has developed a unique style based on the shape of the hexagon, a simple geometric form adopted as his signature. His motifs appear in different media, including on skateboards. For the exhibition he created an original work on a vintage deck made by the Lacadur brand and a ceramic board.

Lacadur skateboard reworked by the artist, 2022.
Photo © Ërell

'Skateboarding is both an essential medium for urban pictorial art and an iconic object within contemporary urban culture. It is an industrial item, produced in large runs, and highly resistant to wear and tear. Asking questions of materials and techniques is a central feature of the way I work; it involves working towards changing the status of the item in a "ready-made" way by designing a series of small, very fragile items manufactured in short runs. When shorn of its initial function, the skateboard becomes a work of art in its own right.'

Ërell

This series of ceramic skateboards was initiated by family streetwear brand La Martelière and produced in collaboration with Buisson Kessler ceramics studio, Apt, France, in 2022.

KEITH HARING

Although not known to be an enthusiastic skater, the king of pop art has often depicted his famous characters perched on top of skateboards. The militant and socially engaged Haring experienced the explosion of hip-hop in the 1980s and saw artists collaborating to create frescos; Dondi White (photographed by the late Ricky Powell), a portrait by Jean-Michel Basquiat and Shepard Fairey, and a skateboard series denouncing the ravages of crack cocaine also became part of this. Haring's work has created a lasting niche for itself within the iconography of skateboarding, thanks to frescos like the one presented to the MACBA in Barcelona. The skateboarding industry has paid significant tribute to his work with skateboard series dedicated to him.

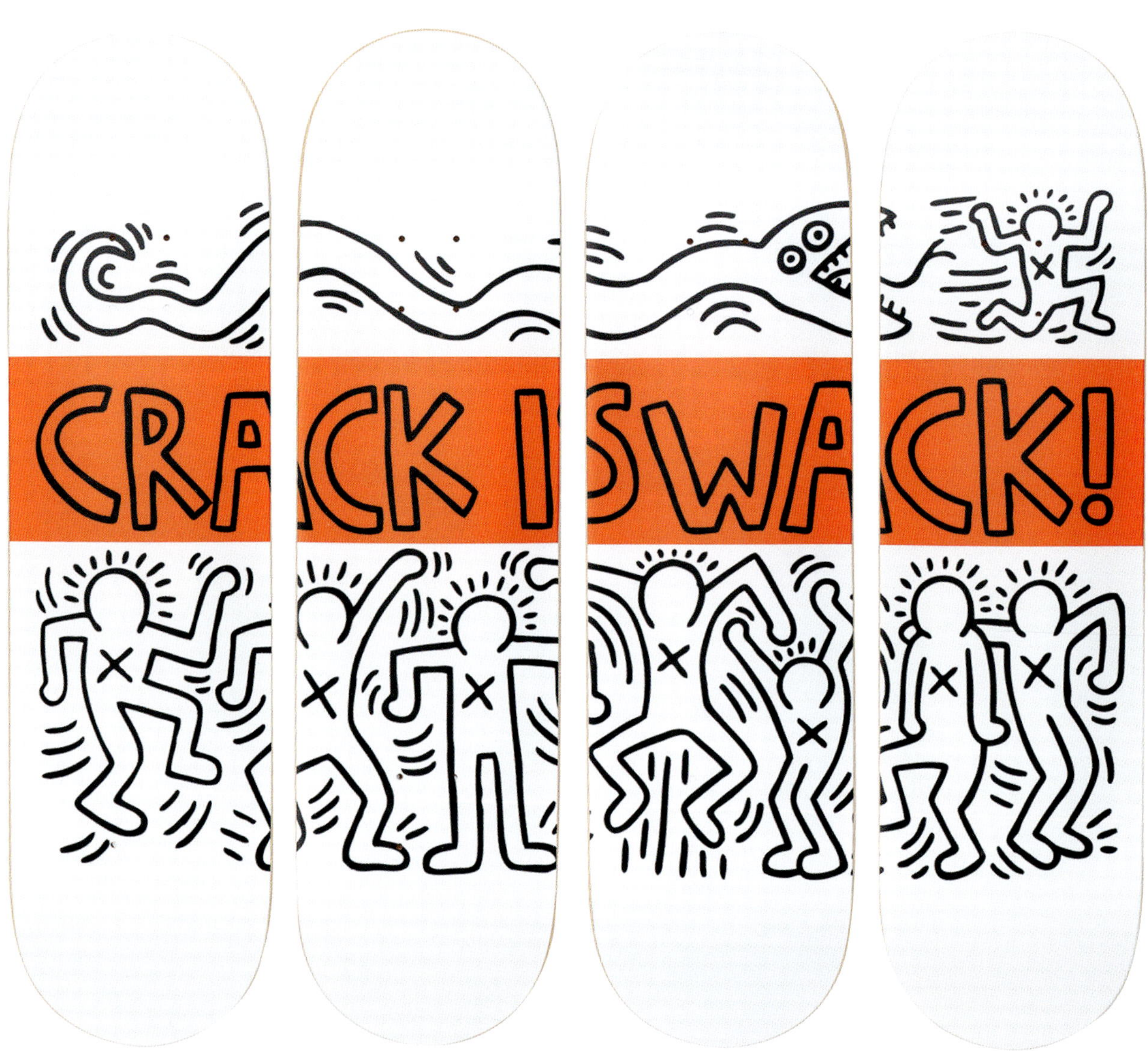

Crack is Wack quadriptych by Keith Haring, manufactured by The Skateroom.

Crack Down, Keith Haring, 1986.

ANDRÉ

Paris, New York, Lisbon and hundreds of other towns and cities around the world have played host to the instantly recognizable Mr. A, a stick figure created by the French artist André Saraiva (known as André), who took his inspiration from the Shadoks, a famous French cartoon series. This grinning alter ego of the artist, invariably shown with his trademark wink, has been attracting the attention of passers-by wherever he has popped up since the 1990s. In the *Ménage à Trois ou Quatre* series shown here, the top-hatted figures are a nod to Paris's famous Le Baron nightclub, which was opened by André in 2004 and eventually closed its doors in 2018.

Smiley triptych produced by The Skateroom.

Photo © Nicolas Scordia

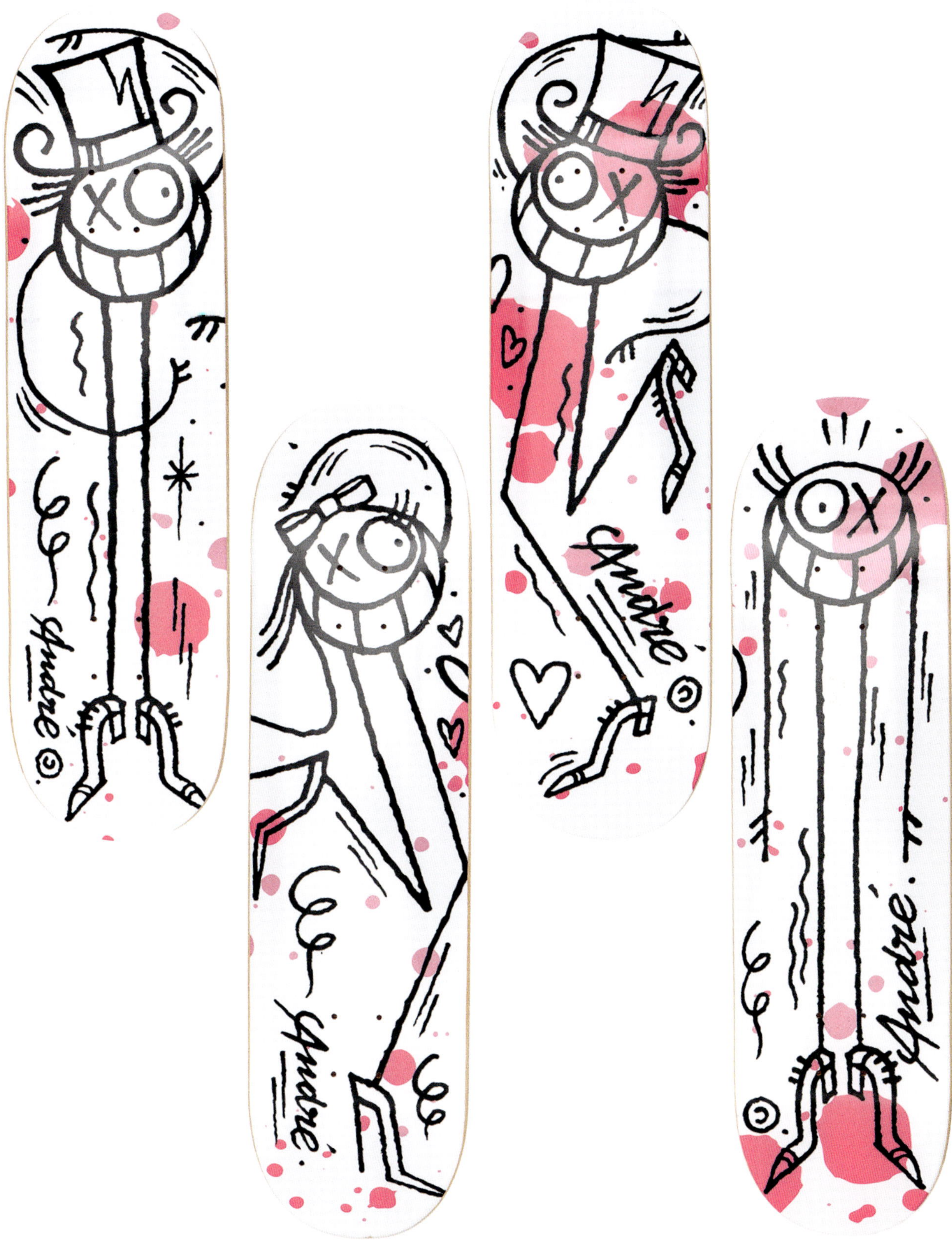

Ménage à Trois ou Quatre, a work created for 1XRUN.
Photo © Nicolas Scordia

ENKI BILAL

The exhibition also featured a triptych by Enki Bilal, a French cartoonist and filmmaker born in Belgrade in 1951. Its graphical style and choice of theme, mixing memory and science fiction, are instantly recognizable. The triptych was debuted in 2021 for the *Reconstrukt?* exhibition organized by the Barbier Gallery. It was the first of three sets of seven portraits making up the *Inclusive Hybrids* series, which focuses on the reinvention of what is human through social, mechanical/digital/technological and transhuman/animal hybridization.

A second collection of boards, bearing the same name as a work by the artist based on an interview with Adrien Rivierre, was produced by Enki Bilal and the Barbier Gallery in 2023 for the *Man is an Accident* exhibition.

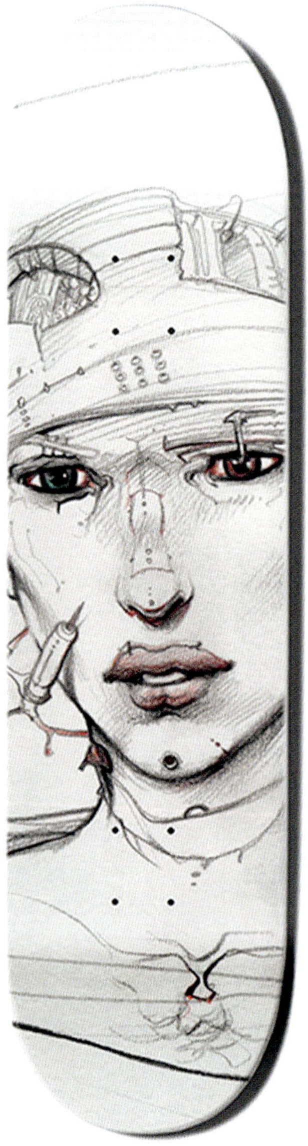
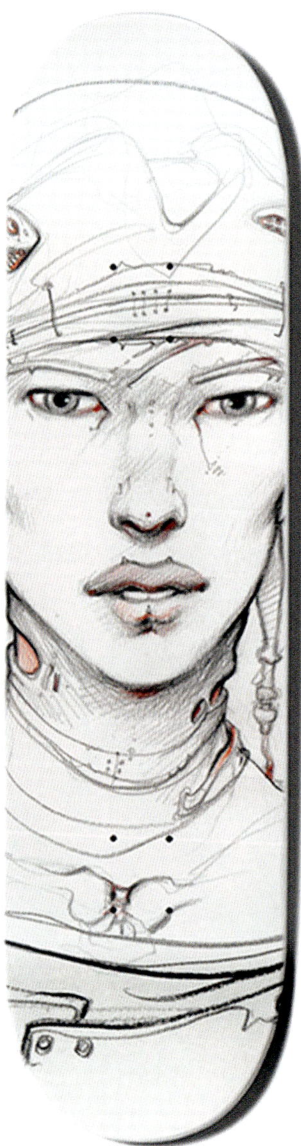

Enki Bilal, triptych, *Reconstrukt?* exhibition, 2021.

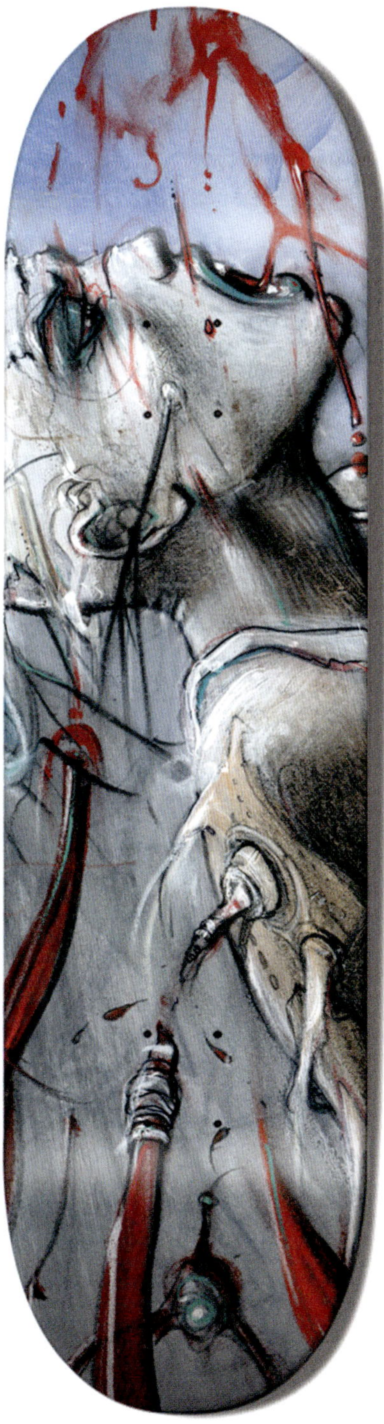

Bilal, set of three boards: *Blindfold Lick*, *Romeo & Juliet*, *Sacha*.

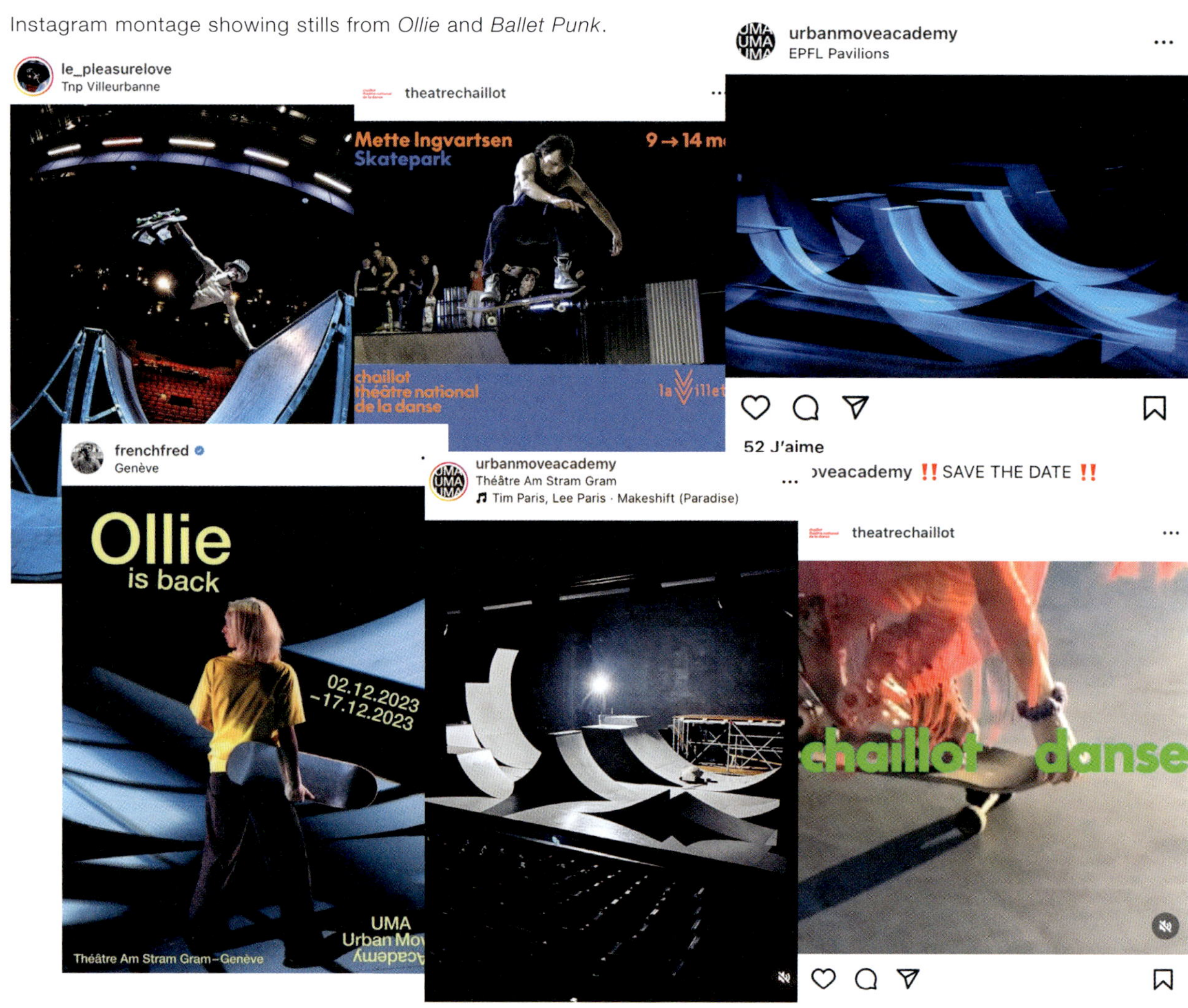

Instagram montage showing stills from *Ollie* and *Ballet Punk*.

'BALLET PUNK' AND 'OLLIE': SKATEBOARDING ON STAGE

Ballet Punk: in May 2023, a skatepark was transformed by some creative magic and in collaboration with the Palais de Chaillot in Paris into a place of true wonder and artistic exploration. Danish choreographer Mette Ingvartsen travelled Europe, presenting a unique show featuring some 20 performers who defied convention and pushed boundaries to create an extraordinary experience.

The skating area, which had been designed in close collaboration with skaters of all levels of experience, became a living artwork on which their movements intertwined like the vivid brushstrokes of paint on a canvas.

Ollie is a cross-disciplinary creation directed by Nicolas Musin that blends skateboarding, parkour, dance, music and poetry. A giant skateboarding ramp on a stage set is used as a backdrop and playground by 15 young artists from Geneva's Urban Move Academy in a liberating and electrifying show expressing their passion, diversity and energy. *Ollie* is an ode to youth, freedom and creativity that defies gravity and convention. It is a waking dream that sweeps us along like a wave.

Instagram montage showing stills from *Wheels and Waves*.

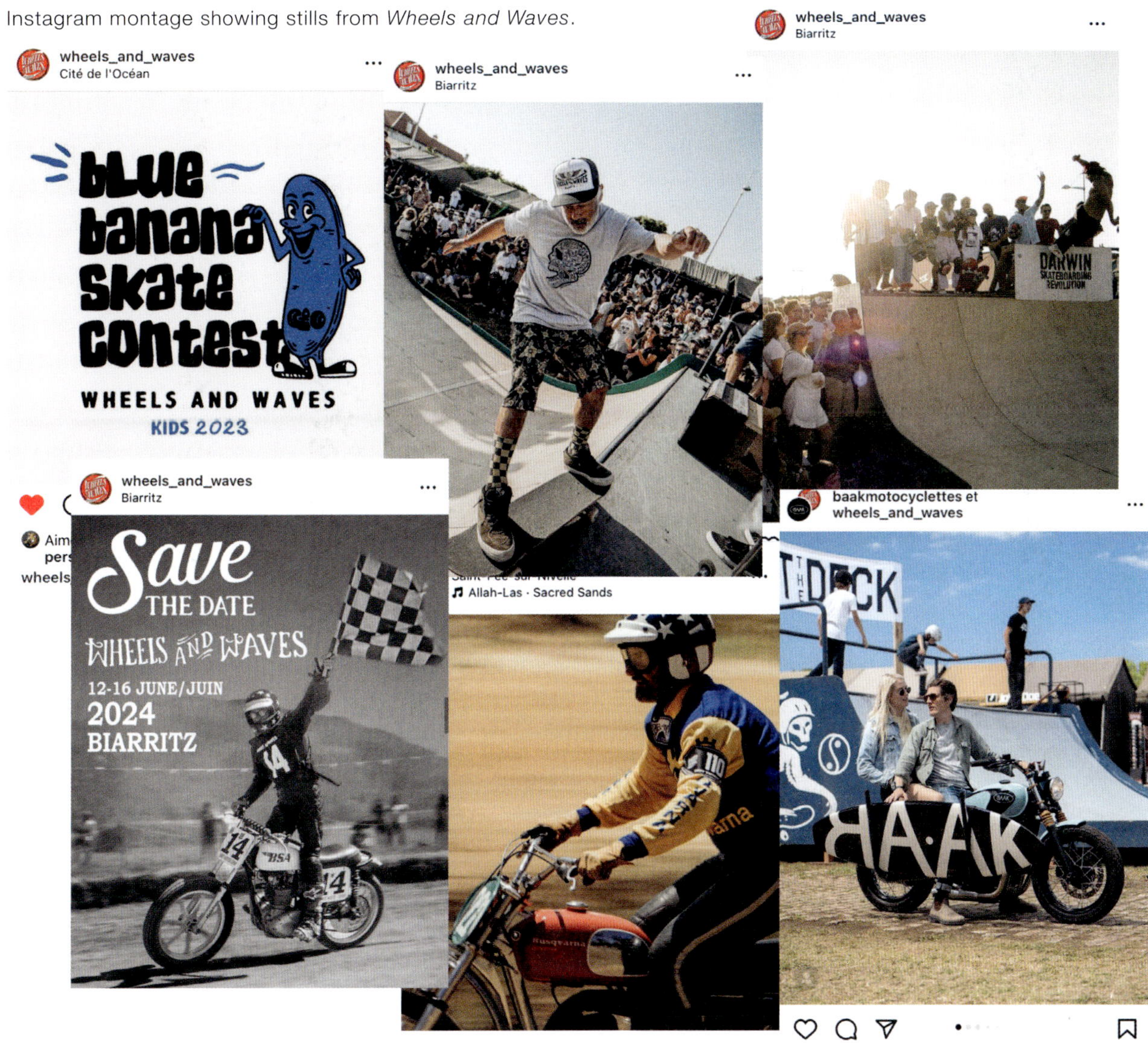

WHEELS AND WAVES FESTIVAL – BIARRITZ – FRANCE

This iconic event is a celebration of surfing, biking and vintage lifestyle and culture. The festival takes place annually, bringing together the worlds of those who glide over both water and asphalt, and it has become an unmissable event for enthusiasts of both cultures, attracting visitors from around the world.

The festival also features an exhibition devoted to skateboarding culture that has become a major contributor to the event's vibrant and creative atmosphere. A wide variety of well-known brands and local manufacturers have stalls showcasing a range of boards, wheels, trucks and other equipment.

Artists from the local and international skate scene present original creations on boards which are genuine works of art, reflecting a spirit and aesthetic unique to skateboarding culture.

This festival is a place where year after year skaters and art lovers can come together to share a common passion and celebrate a unique fusion of skateboarding, motorcycle and surfing cultures.

Sony VX1000 camera.
D.R.

THE IMAGERY OF SKATEBOARDING

Whether seen as a hobby or a spectacular sport, skateboarding is highly visual, attracting the interest of countless photographers – many of whom have focused on it since its earliest days. There is invariably at least one photographer or cameraman in any group of skaters. Skateboard photography has grown from simply preserving precious moments between friends or documenting performances and is now professionalized as a legitimate artistic undertaking with its own history, codes of practice and legendary artists such as J. Grant Brittain and Jim Goodrich.

Footage check >
Photo © Jeff 'Suds' Sudmeier, 2023

Volvic

The American photographer Hugh Holland, who captured the origins of skating in the Southern California of the 1970s, is now hailed as the father of skateboarding photography. His photos, both black-and-white and in colour, epitomize the surfing and hippie spirit of the West Coast of the United States, with skaters of both sexes pushing the envelope of what was then a new sport.

It was around the same time that the American surf photographer Warren Bolster also began to take an interest in skateboarding. He is best known for the spectacular images he achieved by shooting pictures from helicopters and using front or rear deck-mounted cameras.

He was also one of the first to use a fisheye lens for skateboard photography. These wide-angle lenses tend to round out perspective in the image (hence the name, as they are slightly reminiscent of the bulging eye of a fish), creating a style of photography that is now part and parcel of skateboarding imagery.

The essence of this visual identity was consolidated in the 1990s when the Sony VX1000, one of the most popular cameras of the era, was equipped with a wide-angle lens. It soon became the camera of choice and has now itself become an icon of skateboard video making, even featuring on many boards and clothing collections.

One of the difficulties with this kind of photography is the proximity to the skater that is required, and getting the shot can turn into something of a game between photographer and subject.

Magazines and the birth of specialist media have made it much easier for photographers to turn professional and even allowed some to make a name for themselves. This was certainly the case with J. Grant Brittain, who photographed Tony Hawk and has taken some of the most popular images in skating photography. These days, he hosts conferences on the profession, while Tobin Yelland, another big name, has talked about the magic of making a living from his passion, an option that occurred to him only when he sold his first images to a magazine at the age of 15; many of his colleagues tell a similar story.

Jamie Thomas in San Diego. >

Photo © J. Grant Brittain

Canon

Photo taken from a helicopter during a Bones Brigade video shoot, *The Search for Animal Chin*, 1986.
Photo © J. Grant Brittain

ermit
SHOP

Jeff 'Suds' Sudmeier, an American photographer living in Paris, tells the following story of how he began: 'I started to get into photography at high school, around 2012, snapping anything that drew my attention. I would go skating with my friends pretty much every day, which made it a natural subject for me and, as I wasn't the best skater among my friends, I often ended up being the cameraman. I think these years spent behind the lens trained my photographic eye and I never tired of it, as skating is an integral part of my identity. [...] Skateboarding really is one of the best things in the world; not only does it allow you to exercise, you can make friends, challenge yourself and overcome your fears, and it's a creative outlet. Taking photos is a way of giving back what skateboarding has given me, and my aim is to carry on pushing skateboarding to new heights and spreading its influence throughout the world. If my photos contribute to this goal in some way or other, that makes me happy and drives me to continue.'

'My unique 3D photographs show the essence of skateboarding in a visually dynamic and innovative form. Each piece is meticulously crafted by hand, layering multiple prints that are cut with an X-Acto blade and assembled with hot glue. I was inspired by the desire to break free from traditional collages and give viewers an "in-depth" perspective of skating. Through this process, I bring the spots to life, showing the raw energy and creativity of skating in a tangible and captivating manner.'

Jeff 'Suds' Sudmeier

< Max Garcia doing a kickflip at the Erotic Hill Bomb, 2023.
Photo © Jeff 'Suds' Sudmeier

Skateboarding photography has therefore developed its own rules and artists and is primarily the product of a history that has imposed its own customs and language. Capturing a skater's key moment, that fleeting state of grace lasting just a split second, often drives street art photographer and artist Sylvie Barco to tear up the rulebook.

By choosing skateboarding and skateboarders as her subject and taking an outside view, free of the usual constraints of the genre, she manages to capture all these small moments that define both the sport and the lifestyle it has created.

< Sacha Requiem performing a half cab flip, Gare de Lyon, Paris, 2023.
Photo © Jeff 'Suds' Sudmeier

GhlainKlain

SYLVIE BARCO

GANG OF SKATE

Le Dôme

Photo © Sylvie Barco

‘I have been photographing tagged walls all over the world since 1995; every mark tells me something – stories, instincts, feelings, beauty, perhaps – or recounts something about humanity, about what unites us, about the wear and tear of time and the trials and tribulations of life.

It was graffiti that brought me to skateparks. Skating and graffiti have a lot in common – performing a trick or leaving a tag are both ways of expressing yourself, your spontaneity, your freedom.

In 2018, I met three skaters in Spain who took me to the city of Gandia, to a skatepark where metal ramps and half-pipes perform a vital function: promoting connection. I was fascinated by the relationship that everyone had with falling, and by the meeting of body and board, which attract one another like the two poles of a magnet; it was there that I began the *G*O*S* (short for Gang Of Skate) series. I also discovered skateboarding, which translates an entire, expressive language, the interior monologue of young people in search of self-expression and freedom. I grabbed it with both hands as a witness to my own emotions.

In Paris, I was interested in the skaters at Le Dôme, the forecourt of the Palais de Tokyo, which has become an essential, iconic space for skaters where street furniture is not an obstacle but a means to perform, representing the possibility of a stylish trick. The city is like a laboratory, where every corner, every nook and cranny is an invitation to probe and explore, to be challenged. This place is the perfect reflection of the skaters’ identity: committed free spirits. My approach has now become distanced from classic skater photography to concentrate on additional associated aspects; if skateboarding derives from surfing, I too am waiting to “catch the right wave” to trigger my shutter.

There is a semi-mystical way of thinking running throughout *G*O*S* that redefines urban space, transcending the act of falling and sublimating the balance of the body. Their animal vitality measures the extent to which skateboarding communicates and disseminates its rebellious harmony. Their philosophy explores profound aspects of existence: memory, heritage, the place of women, the affirmation of the self – these realities show that skateboarding is also a pure allegory of life.’

GANG
OF
SKATE
HELLO
my name is

URBAN RHYTHMS

Taggers and skaters leave their mark, whether with a spray can or a board. They invade public space, their rebellious attitude distracting and asserting itself as the spirit of true independence, resisting the laws of normality.

Marked with garish streaks of paint and burnt rubber, the fluid concrete shapes explore another aspect of creativity: the urban environment of cities is packed with abandoned places, deserted spaces where these two faces of invention emerge. At the foot of a wall or in full flight, these stars of freedom are a hymn to life, inviting us to see the world through new eyes, to engage with difference, with discovery, and an alternative form of inspiration.

Together graffiti and skating disrupt and shake things up – there are cries of rebellion, howls of joy, striking out into the void of an organized social system, with paint dripping and boards clattering. A slam dunk of freedom, an explosion of expressivity. It is noisy and fast-paced: worlds merge, values are enriched.

This is street culture.

BORING

les vagues de l'asphalte
GANG OF SKATE

GOSSES DU BÉTON
Ton

FUJI 200

carlos
aebi

PLANCHE N° ....
SUJET..L..'instant..Kimi
DATE 2018........ PHOTOGRAPHE...................

There were three skateboarders that day, young and wild, gliding by on their boards. There was that Spo

And finally, there was a brutal light that played over the texture of their bodies, and the damp warmt

leader of the pack, was proudly showing off his first tattoos. His cryptograms and secret runes told tale

The wheels left behind a few marks on the hot concrete, proof that they had passed by. That they had s

The energy of skateboarding makes you more alive, filling you with strength and offering the possibility

Slogging away, falling over, believing, getting back up, breaking things: it's a unique experience that m

Maybe anything is (or will be) possible; skateboarding is all about flying high and making dreams come

are, which the oppressive heat had ensured was deserted.

endered shone in their faces. Stripped to the waist, Kimi, the

, of his life.

ped, flown – that they had risked their necks.

pletely different take on the things in your life.

stronger, more authentic and more creative.

n the craziest ones.

THE SPIRIT OF TONI

Where Gandia ends, the TONI skatepark begins. This is the edge of *terra incognita*, scorched by the boiling heat of Spain, where building and construction are challenging. This is where the last high-rise blocks at the outskirts of the city keep watch over walls covered in spray paint. Venturing beyond risks becoming lost in abandoned expanses of land straddling highways and dried-up riverbeds. This area is perfectly integrated into local life, and the soul of a community flows through it like a breath of oxygen.

There's a mix of all ages and the atmosphere is contagious. The half-pipes monopolize space, demanding control and dictating movement – obstacles that require greater technical skill. The rocking of the boards numbs the city, the regular and repetitive rattle no longer a din but soothing, a remedy for young people already tired of a life with uncertain horizons.

TONI comes alive during summer nights, when the concrete cools down.

Huge truck tyres and cement blocks are no longer obstacles to be negotiated by BMX riders but instead a stage on which anyone is free to create their own story. Games are invented, children hide and first stirrings of emotions are hidden out of sight. Young people are figures in a compelling, captivating space that is entirely out of the ordinary, where life is joyful, where light dazzles – even in the half-shadows. This off beat setting gives the space a unique atmosphere, an immersive visual style inviting escape into an almost imaginary world.

1955
RUDA
PONS

LE DÔME
CULTURE

Le Dôme is both a legend and a culture shock; it is the skaters' landmark space, their territory, a sea of smooth concrete. Skaters come from far and wide to glide along under the watchful eye of the stone nymphs.

They deconstruct classical art, creating an off-piste route through the city, testing their ability to disrupt the frontiers of genre. They force unexpected encounters as they skip from steps to railings, from walls to benches, moving between cultural and counter-cultural history. This is a skate space that pulses with life, overflowing with adrenaline at every point, where the rattle of the boards echoes through the city like a rallying cry.

Le Dôme is an appropriation of urban space with its own customs and codes, a context that creates a more chaotic atmosphere. It involves dealing with the city and its unpredictability, and danger is all the more real. Skaters are confronted with different obstacles that constantly force them to be creative. Sometimes recklessness is the only option. It's as if the fountains have had a tiny sip of their anxiety, the steps have stilled their panic and the sculptures have frozen their fear.

The social groups are recognizable at Le Dôme, with generations X, Y and Z happily living alongside each other, making the experience more social and painting a portrait of a complex society. They use the space like a psychologist's couch, a listening ear, an observer of journeys and different lifestyles. The wise among them protect the DNA of the space while the new bring fresh energy. Le Dôme should never disappear, it is a spark of explosive expression with many echoes.

What links TONI and Le Dôme is a way of being – skaters have a particular attitude, similar approaches. Even if they are huddled together in a group in a corner, the sound of rap can often be heard drifting from a speaker with the smell of hash hovering in the air. Voices rise above the noise of the boards along with the chink of beer bottles. Food is shared and T-shirts removed as tricks are discussed and deconstructed.

Skaters share the same alternative culture that cultivates their uniqueness as a group, expands their imagination and opens them up to freedom. Even when the group is dispersed, it remains united by a sense of belonging to the same community, one that exists and evolves by sharing advice and contributing to their creativity. Together, each one skates for themself, striving to outdo each other yet always expressing the spirit of the group.

IN MEMORIAM

One particular portrait tagged on the wall of the skatepark leaves no one unmoved. It is the youthful face of Toni Medina, a skater who committed suicide. His death hit the group hard and they wanted to pay a powerful tribute to him to remind us of the fragility of life. The features of his face, fixed on the wall, force us to explore the complexity of what it means to be human. Skating becomes an invitation to come together, to share, to remember – a window opening onto the most intense of emotions, a reminder of the need to unite to record the living memory of experiences.

REBELLIOUS HARMONY

Welcome to Skateland! An independent state with its own rules and regulations, where its citizens communicate with their own hand signals, speak their own language and have their own unique, cool style. They are united by rituals that strengthen their bonds even as they alienate outsiders.

The skaters have built a micro-society in which their culture and lifestyle meld into a coherent whole. Being part of this is the source of their identity and is proof that a community can exist in an anonymous and impersonal urban environment.

Gathered together in the group, each is both coach and spectator, a duality that clearly defines the soul of a skater. There is no competition, no winner or loser, just a search for a style, for self-expression. Everyone knows everyone – if not very well then from afar by sight. Strangers don't stay strangers for long. They bond, supporting one another and pushing each individual to reach new heights; no one seeks to dominate or lead, there is just the collective, tuned in to a common frequency.

These asphalt warriors have found their Promised Land in the streets, a space time continuum where there are no rules. Here, they can experience ecstasy and face failure without pretence or artifice. Everything is shared among them with raw sincerity in a universe that belongs to them, a parallel world where reality fades away and limits are pushed back. This is a group of 'individuals' in which each skater has to find their place in order to get their own particular shot of adrenaline.

TATTOOED CONCRETE

Attempting a trick means braving cuts and bruises, scars and even the occasional fractured limb. So many brands inspire the skaters, while the scars are like another kind of tattoo. How will life reinterpret these constant falls, from which they always seem to pick themselves up?

With bravery and perseverance, even the most hazardous move can always be mastered. Little by little, the skater will find the perfect balance to triumph in the trick. The skin takes the hit like the bumper on a car, the body takes flight, forming shapes in a poetic urban ballet. There is always something beautiful, a certain grace, in every fall, and while the asphalt may be a reminder of the harshness of existence, the act of falling helps to maintain the momentum of life. It makes us go higher and further, like dancing with pain in order to conquer rage.

Skaters learn how to fall, positioning their bodies perfectly as they roll heavily on the concrete. A fall is never a failure, merely an unavoidable step on the road to better understanding, to ultimate success. It's a process of apprenticeship, a constant struggle between sensations of pleasure and pain. A successful outcome always seems to be in exchange for a tumble, a price that has to be paid.

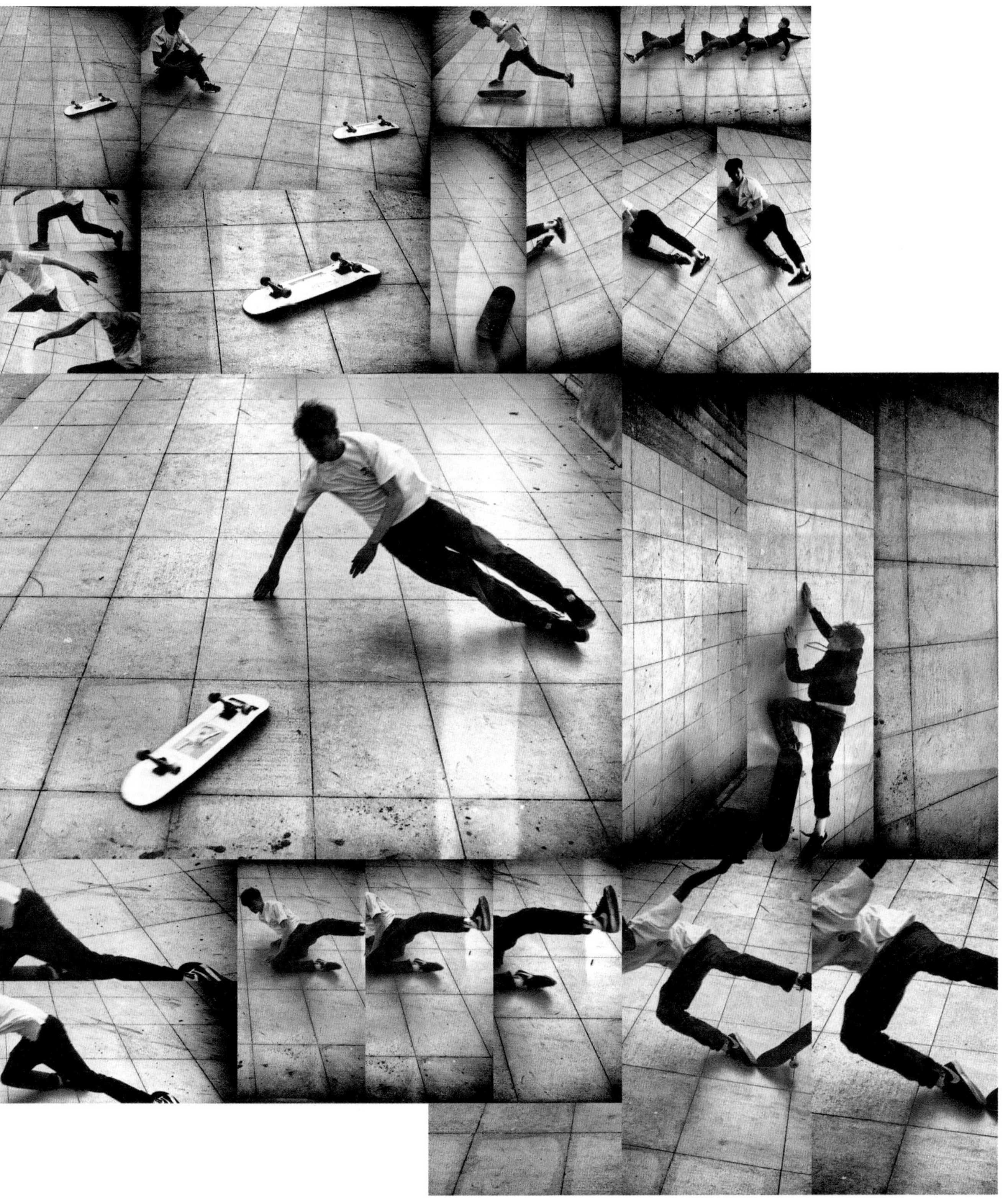

You fall, you pick yourself up with a groan, and you continue to push the envelope. It's a risk, a challenge, a moment of pain, a cry of joy that you accept, that makes you stronger and more determined.

STYLISH
TRICK

Skaters have their own unique body language. Their warm bodies against the cold of the concrete are an extension of their self-expression, and each welcomes the other in total communion. This is an inseparable whole, a melding of material and form. They know how to outwit the imperfections of urban space, exploiting every nook and cranny, to reveal their personalities and create their identities.

Caught against the light for a split second, leaping and defying vertical space, a magic spell is cast. Frozen in time by the camera lens, their athleticism creates other stories – a bird spreading its wings, feet on a razor's edge, an electric shock... Everything, down to the last fingertip, comes to life only to be fixed in time; nothing is left to chance.

The contorted appearance of the posture becomes pure choreography, exact and perfect. The mechanics of the physical, a body in perpetual motion, a wave spreading through the void. This organic fusion is a physical and emotional spectacle between the skater and their environment – an urban ballet accompanied by the chaotic, incessant, rhythmic clatter of the boards.

The unpredictable sound of rattling wheels is in perfect time with the tricks, a true improvisation between harmony and discord that is magnetic in its effect. When the skating stops and the park is empty, all that is left are phantom sounds and we search in vain for these free spirits, now departed, who have bequeathed to the city a living energy that is so vibrant and expressive.

SECRETS

Skating is an adolescent space, a social sphere for a younger generation that is predominantly male. Women are very much present, but, like an audience in the background, they observe and support – they get close but most do not skate. However, female skaters do exist and they too use the board as a means to assert themselves, a lever to push their own limits, a way to express their power, a way to live in freedom.

Women can and indeed do become asphalt warriors too, but it takes double the effort first to free themselves from, and then to shatter, all expectations, and to take up their rightful place in the skating community. Their communities are inclusive and egalitarian. They unite in solidarity under the banner of a collective that fosters their existence and above all creates a warm and welcoming environment where kindness and mutual assistance prevail. They create their own small groups where the door is always open and each can progress at their own pace. These verge on the political, encouraging the protection of minorities, gender issues and the environment, a declaration of strength and determination. The women are finding self-expression and rebellion.

BETESGA
A
Coeur
VAILLANT

SANTA CRUZ

SKATE

LIVING MEMORY

Skating heritage forms an invisible connection between skaters that in the parks finds tangible, physical form whatever the surface, whether asphalt or metal. The board unites the skaters in a close bond that never breaks. It is a means of communication. Experts mingle with newbies and guide them by example or a few words of advice, given in an informal and collaborative spirit. In this quasi-ideal system mistakes are even encouraged and progress applauded. It all adds up to a spirit of invention and perseverance, with skaters tirelessly striving to surpass themselves and especially to rise to the challenge. They have their values and their own mindset, sharing in a complete lesson in life passed on through their interactions with each other.

Just as old VHS clips, over the years, eventually find their way onto the internet, this is where traditions and tales have been shared to create skateboarding's sacred heritage. It's an intergenerational process that helps to expand the sport. The oldest riders, who have watched skateboarding evolve from its very beginnings, swap stories, remembering key moments and skating icons, preserving the essence of skating, while still allowing it to evolve. The new generation is just as inspired as its predecessor, but brings a breath of fresh air and a different perspective, creating a link between the different eras, with new approaches that also transcend borders and cultures. They have established a universal language, one without words or frontiers, in a spirit of mutual comprehension among riders from around the world as they identify, connect and share experiences with one another. While passing on knowledge enriches memory, in skating it is a passionate process of sharing that never ceases to inspire and reflect the most ambitious dreams.

A SIGNATURE

The style expresses the skaters' ideals. The baggy clothing, blackened by friction against the asphalt, seems shapeless at first glance, but transforms in an instant into a second skin, flattening against the body as it gathers speed, each fold a creative gesture, or billowing out as the fabric takes on a sculptural quality. It smells of cement, an authentic silent witness to their skills. Tears, holes, faded cloth; just like the riders, skate clothes bear the scars acquired from gliding through the city. The crowning glory of the whole outfit, quite literally, is an American baseball cap.

The rebelliousness of the kings of the tarmac is reflected in their sunglasses which accentuate their mystery and catch the eye. A backpack, keeper of all their secrets, accompanies them wherever they go. The belt is sometimes just a length of wire. Tattoos read like an exclusive alphabet, an indelible branding to demonstrate affiliation. Music also contributes to the scene, adding sound to this urban tableau as it escapes in a trickle from earbuds. Shapes, graffiti and stickers are thrown around like brushstrokes. It is not just to do with appearance but is a battle between soul and city, between individuality and belonging, each rider stamping their own personality, their own story, on the asphalt, creating a living fresco that engages the audience. This self-expression can only raise questions about our own freedom of spirit.

SKATEPARK
HUNTINGTON BEACH, CALIFORNIA
HOUSE OF
GAME OVER
OFF THE WALL
VANS

IF IT'S TOO LOUD YOU'RE TOO OLD
GO AWAY!
MELPOMENE
BE THE ORIGINAL
turbo
POWER and RESPONSE

FREEWHEELING

The skateboard is far more than its 34 or so inches (86cm) – it is truly an extension of the skater, revealing all their inner strength. It guides the rider towards resilience, becoming the light of their soul and the shadow of their desires. The board is a vector of their thoughts and actions. As soon as they set foot upon it, the world is transformed into a constant striving to strike the perfect balance between stability and perpetual motion. The maple wood veneers of the board sculpt the perception of perseverance as the embodiment of the eternal desire to overcome challenge.

Seven layers of wood that together express individuality and identity. The choice of board unites, forms brotherhoods and breaches borders. It challenges the inaccessible, creating a world in which the only rule is that there are none. It invites the rider to explore hidden dreams, to push back the boundaries of life. The board makes the skater more alive; it is their war cry, their voice. It glides gracefully, in perfect communion with the asphalt. In a seamless interaction with the environment, the board is unique in making a playground of the city's panorama. The board is also sound – as the skaters take off, the shock of the wheels' impact on the ground fills the air. It is a hypnotic, repetitive din, a rolling rattle with a metallic edge, a sound with a mesmerizing rhythm revealing the fusion of bodies with concrete – like surfing asphalt waves.

MAIN CRA

Supreme
Supreme
N°13
DOME
PARIS

'I became a skater thanks to a little bit of cash that my grandmother gave me for Christmas. I like challenging places to skate, like steps, rails, ledges – anything big attracts me because I love the feeling of adrenaline. I feel free on my board, I can go anywhere, I can go faster, I can grind, I feel this piece of metal under my feet which is in contact with something that in essence wasn't even made for that purpose. Whenever I get a bit angry, I get my board and I go skating and I ride hard; I'm going to fall, but that will clear my head – skateboarding is sort of my therapy.' **Gaspard**

'I'm an embalmer and I work in a mortuary; I also rap and I do tattooing, but what I like most is skateboarding. My worst memory of doing a trick? I passed out in mid-air, broke my collarbone and a part of my shoulder blade, dislocated my shoulder and cracked a rib. I can see myself skateboarding until my body can't take it anymore. However, my dream is to get better and better and to create my own skating brand.' **Bata**

'I sometimes feel frustrated when I skate, because some moments are harder than others, but to be honest, we ride to disconnect; it's being able to find an hour or two every day to ride. That helps a lot to recharge the batteries and calm the mind. The feeling of clearing your head comes from a sense of freedom, because this is a sport where you really can do whatever you like, you don't have a list of rules to follow, you can ride how you want.' **Jan**

00:00:00

• REC

'I was born into skateboarding; my parents had a skate shop when I was little and I had my first board by the age of six. This was the golden age of skating. When I skate now, I'm completely alone, there's just me and my board, nothing else. It's freedom! I'll never stop.' **Kimi**

'The primary thing I feel about skateboarding is the freedom to be wherever you want, whenever you want, at any time – there's no law, there aren't any rules. It's on the streets, it's not just in the gym, and it's creative – creativity and freedom are the only two things I find interesting in sport, and culture too. Being with people, meeting up, swapping notes, it's so easy to reach the people around me. You meet people who are massively different from one another, and there's no need to be super formal to make real connections.' **Lorène**

'Skateboarding is still considered a relatively new and niche pastime in Morocco, but a community of enthusiastic skaters is slowly growing, and there are skateparks and events that are organized to promote the sport. There are far more male skaters than female as it is sometimes thought of as a "sport for boys", but associations have been founded to promote it to girls. Despite a certain amount of prejudice, skateboarding is growing in popularity in Morocco and is becoming increasingly accepted.' **Salma**

A few skateboarding terms

Backside and frontside • In skateboarding, these terms are used to describe the position of the skater and the direction of rotation of the board. The term *frontside* means that the skater is facing in the direction of the rotation of the board while *backside* means the skater has their back to it. These terms are also used to describe turns and tricks; for turns, the direction of rotation is *frontside* when the beginning of the turn exposes the front of the body and you can see what is happening; the direction of rotation is *backside* when the turn exposes the back of the body and the skater cannot clearly see what is going on. The direction of rotation is often simply written as initials (BS or FS).

Board • Also known as a 'deck', usually made of maple wood.

Bowl • A skateboarding style involving a succession of tricks that follow curved cement walls. It is also the name given to the place where such tricks are performed, as this looks like a curved bowl.

Contest • A skating competition.

Curbs • Solid skating elements similar to a bench with edges along which a skater can grind or slide.

Fakie • A technique that involves rolling backwards, while facing forwards.

Flat • Skateboarding on the ground.

Goofy • A skateboard stance in which the right foot is placed on the board and the left is used to push; this is the opposite of 'regular'.

Nose • The concave part at the front of the board.

New-school • The new approach; in other words, all the tricks that appeared during the Rodney Mullen era, such as the kickflip, heelflip, 360 flip and their various incarnations.

Old-school • Refers to the traditional style of skateboarding with tricks like a boneless or no comply shove-it.

Pop • This term is used to describe the height achieved during a jump or trick, from the verb 'to pop', which refers to the act of slamming the rear of the board against the ground to propel it into the air.

Pro model • A device used by skateboard brands to target an audience by manufacturing a product dedicated to their best-loved athletes. This will often be a board or shoes on which the name of a professional skater appears; in skateboarding, a pro model is also far more indicative that a rider has turned professional than any competition victory.

Regular • The left foot is positioned on the front of the board and the right is used to push; this is the opposite of 'goofy'.

Set-up • A complete skateboard with board or 'deck', trucks and wheels.

Skatepark • Dedicated place for skateboarding.

Slides • When a part of the skateboard glides along a curb or a rail, such as in a tailslide, noseslide or boardslide.

Stance • Position of a skater's feet on the board; there are two main stances, regular and goofy.

Street • A skateboarding style that involves adapting to urban architecture, either directly on a street or in a skatepark made up of elements that reproduce street furniture such as rails and curbs.

Switch • A skateboarding technique that involves skating with the opposite foot, i.e. if you are normally regular, your right foot will now be at the front, and vice versa for a goofy skater.

Tail • Refers to the concave section at the back of the board.

Tricks • Acrobatic jumps and turns; there are several, but one of the best known is the ollie (the name given to a simple jump when the push against the ground is applied from the back of the board; popping the front, or nose, of the board, is called a nollie). A trick can be performed either fakie or switch.

Truck • The metal assembly that is used to attach the wheels to the board.

Biographies

Sylvie Barco

Having graduated from the *Icart Photo* school of photography in Paris in 1996, Sylvie Barco has been expressing her fascination with the imagery of walls for 25 years, releasing three photo series: an abstract and curated collection in *Lomoscope*, a collation of street details in *Chaos*, and the universal language of street art incorporated into *Wall Street*.

A chance encounter in Spain in 2018 led her to a new project entitled *G*O*S* (an abbreviation of Gang Of Skate). During work on her *Wall Street* project, she created immersive collages of photographs of walls and skateboards, capturing their narrative and poetic essence.

Her work has been hailed by Mister Freeze, Grimaud Art Urbain and Le Strokar, and 'wall art' has become for her an introspective territory within which she can express her emotions. In the studio, her *Kingdom* series explores the tribal choreography and hip-hop style of 'krumping', while *Instagraff* enhances her wall photography with stencils.

In 2022, she was given control of a 50-ft (15-m) wall with the first immersive *G*O*S* collage at the *Art of Skate* exhibition at Fluctuart.

In 2022, Sylvie Barco was selected as a member of France's *100 Women of Culture*.

Nicolas Barthélémy

Nicolas Barthélémy has been passionate about the skateboarding universe (skating and skating culture) since adolescence, and he loves to share his enthusiasm for the images, music and art he has discovered and explored through this interest. He is a regular speaker at Mauna Kea, an association that organizes events and festivals specializing in board sports. Whether on his board, on video or in the stories and anecdotes told in this book, Nicolas Barthélémy has a love for everything that skateboarding has brought him, and he hopes to share this enthusiasm with readers.

Philippe Danjean

Philippe Danjean has been collecting urban and contemporary art for 20 years. His discoveries everywhere from New York to Berlin via Los Angeles have brought together a host of works with links to the urban scene. Galleries, auction rooms and art fairs have also allowed him to support collectors in their search for new talent. He is the co-creator of Spray (an urban art collection organized as a club) and has curated several exhibitions in France and abroad. He has taught cultural management at ICART Paris, where he is coordinator for an MBA in international art marketing, and at HEC. He was co-organizer (with Stéphane Madoeuf) of the *Art of Skate* exhibition in Paris in 2022 and collaborates regularly on projects with the Musée en Herbe in Paris and Little Beaux-Arts in Lyon.

Stéphane Madoeuf

Stéphane Madoeuf, who has long been a massive fan of board sports, graffiti and music, began collecting vinyl, posters and flyers in 1990 before expanding his interests to urban culture in the 2000s. After working in marketing at various companies, he now teaches at HEC Paris, where he runs courses relating to digital culture, entrepreneurism and art. He has initiated several projects and helped to promote artists via various exhibitions in France and abroad. Co-curating the *Art of Skate* exhibition at Fluctuart allowed him to showcase a part of his collection and inspire a new generation of collectors and skaters. Stéphane Madoeuf's collections, in particular those exhibited at Station F, have always been intended for installation in art centres or places open to the general public and the younger generation in particular. He is committed to exposing as many people as possible to art and continues to leave a lasting mark at the intersection of digital innovation and artistic expression.

Acknowledgments

Thank you, first of all, to all the artists, photographers, associations and institutions who have been involved with this book.

Thanks to:

- Nicolas Barthélémy, who provided us with advice and support in drafting this book; his expertise and talent were invaluable assets in completing it;
- Nicolas Laugero Lasserre and all the Fluctuart teams for the faith they had and the assistance they provided during the *Art of Skate* exhibition which started this project, ICART students for the outreach they carried out, and the 50,000 visitors who came to the exhibition in Paris;
- Jim Zbinden at the Geneva Skateboard Museum for his advice and for giving us access to iconic skateboards;
- the skaters, skateshops, skateparks, associations and clubs who have helped to popularize skateboarding culture;
- Kimi, Jan, Bata, Martin and the gang for their inspiration and creativity;
- Sophie from the Realaxe association, Lorène and Salma, who shared their talents and enriched this book, and the queer skating collective Slayte.

Last but not least, many thanks to our editor, Sabine Bledniak, and to Pierre-Olivier Planty for their faith and valuable help, and to Sylvain Enguehard for his keen eye and the work he contributed to this book.

Thanks to our families and friends for the support they give every day, which has breathed life into these pages.

Big thanks to:
Alain Weill, Alexandre Charlaix, Alex & Big Mess Skateboarding, Anne-José Beuzelin, Antiz, Agathe Wullepit, Learn and Skate Association, the Realaxe Association, Antoine Dubreuil, Chloé Bernard, Chris Dale, Christian Omodéo, Collection Spray, Cyril Pitet, Cyrille Gouyette, David Manzic, Enki Bilal, Erell, Etnies, Fred Ferrant, Gabriel Renault, Hangar Darwin, Harvey Brepson, Ian Rodgers, Iker Murone, Iron Distribution, Jean-Claude Geraud, Jean-Michel Pailhon, Jean-Baptiste Barbier, Jeff 'Suds' Sudmeier, Jim Goodrich, Jim Zbinden & The Geneva Skateboard Museum, Joachim Romain, Julien Bachelier, Julien Bécaud, J. Grant Brittain, the Barbier Gallery, Laurent Janouin, Léo Valls, the teams at the Musée en Herbe, Leyla Madoeuf, Maellys Madoeuf, Magenta Skateboards, Marco, Martha Cooper, Martin Leclair, Matu Ostoja, Mauna Kea Skim Club, Mélanie Tresch, Mucem (Marseilles), Nicolas Jacquemin, Nicolas Scordia, Renaud Marion, Robin Briard, Samuel Bucciacchio, Montauban skatepark, Hangar Darwin skatepark, The Smithsonian Institution, Soy Panday, Sylvain Ponserre, Théo Bardyn, Thibault Le Nours, Thomas Laisney, Tim Clément, Twelve Consulting, V7 Distribution, Yahel Galtier.

Éditions Alternatives would like to extend warm thanks to the artists and photographers who have kindly contributed images for this book.

Some of the items illustrating this book are from private collections:
Philippe Danjean: pp 11, 14, 17, 25, 28, 44-45, 46, 47, 58, 59, 63, 78, 79, 82, 102, 140, 152, 153, 158
Stéphane Madoeuf: pp 80, 83, 95 (middle board), 140, 141,150, 154
Strend: pp 146, 148
Barbier Gallery: p. 155

Originally published by Éditions Gallimard, collection Alternatives,
5, rue Gaston-Gallimard, Paris VIIe, France.

First published in Great Britain in 2025 by Cassell,
an imprint of Octopus Publishing Group Ltd
Carmelite House
50 Victoria Embankment
London EC4Y 0DZ
www.octopusbooks.co.uk
www.octopusbooksusa.com

An Hachette UK Company
www.hachette.co.uk

The authorised representative in the EEA is Hachette Ireland,
8 Castlecourt Centre, Castleknock Road, Castleknock,
Dublin 15, D15 YF6A, Ireland (email: info@hbgi.ie)

Distributed in the US by Hachette Book Group
1290 Avenue of the Americas, 4th and 5th Floors
New York, NY 10104

Distributed in Canada by Canadian Manda Group
664 Annette St., Toronto, Ontario, Canada M6S 2C8

ISBN 978-1-78840-575-1

A CIP catalogue record for this book is available from the British Library.

Printed and bound in Poland.

10 9 8 7 6 5 4 3 2 1